Online Shopper's Survival Guide

Order Anything, Anywhere, Anytime

Online Shopper's Survival Guide

Jacquelyn Lynn

Entrepreneur.
Press

Editorial Director: Jere L. Calmes
Cover Design: Barry T. Kerrigan
Production and Composition: Eliot House Productions

Library of Congress Cataloging-in-Publication Data
Lynn, Jacquelyn.
    Online shopper's survival guide/by Jacquelyn Lynn.
      p.   cm.
    ISBN 1-59918-024-3 (9781599180243 : alk. paper)
    1. Teleshopping—Guidebooks. 2. Shopping—Computer network resources—
Guidebooks. I. Title.
TX335.L96 2006
658.8'72—dc22   2006000800

Printed in Canada
12 11 10 09 08 07 06   10 9 8 7 6 5 4 3 2 1

Contents

Acknowledgments.............................. xi
Preface xiii

Part I
Introduction to Online Buying

Chapter 1

How Did We Get Here? 3

The More Things Change, the More
   They Stay the Same 4
The Evolution of E-Commerce 6
Why Shop Online? 7
Ways to Buy Online 8

Online Shopper's

Chapter 2

Online Shopping Basics 11

Evaluating an Online Seller 12

What Do Others Think About the Seller? 16

The Purchasing Process 20

Paying for Online Purchases 23

Money-Saving Tips 28

Chapter 3

From Teenagers to Seniors:
Generational Issues 33

Young People 33

Seniors 35

Age Doesn't Matter 35

Part II

Let's Go Shopping

Chapter 4

Online Auctions 39

How Online Auctions Work 42

Finding What You Want 43

The Seller Might Have Something Else You Want 45

Misspellings Can Spell B-A-R-G-A-I-N-S 46

Imitation Is the Highest Form of Flattery 46

Don't Re-Create the Wheel 47

Do You Know from Whom You're Buying? 48

Can You Get a Good Look? 50

You've Searched, You've Found It,
  You Want It—What Now? 51

Placing Bids at the Last Second 54

You Won—What Happens Next? 55

When Things Go Wrong 56

Chapter 5

The Good, the Bad, and the Bargains of Online Auctions **57**

An Infinite Variety 58

Avoid the Battle of a Bidding War 60

Don't Wait to Resolve a Problem 61

Don't Blame the Seller for Your Mistakes 61

Chapter 6

Finding What You Want Online **63**

How Search Engines Work 64

How to Use Online Search Engines 66

Shopping the Shopping Search Engines 68

Chapter 7

What You Can't—or Shouldn't—Buy Online **71**

Online Auction Sites Have the Most Rules............... 72

Buying Weapons Online 73

Online Sales of Tobacco Products and Alcoholic Beverages . . 73

Chapter 8

Buying from Foreign Countries................ **75**

International Payments and Foreign Currencies 76

How Will the Seller Ship? 76

Customs, Duty, and Taxes 77

Chapter 9

Consumer Protection Issues **79**

Set Up an E-Mail Address Exclusively
for Online Shopping 80

Paying with a Credit Card Is the Safest Way to Shop........ 81

When Things Go Wrong 83

Dealing with Credit Card Billing Errors 87

Be a Responsible Online Shopper........................ 89

Don't Get Spied On. 91
Secure All Your Electronic Devices 95

Chapter 10

Frauds and Scams **97**
Identity Theft. 98
Sex Products, Fake Designer Watches, Pharmaceuticals,
  Million-Dollar Business Opportunities, and More. 101
Common Frauds and Scams 101
Tips for Avoiding Scams and Cons. 111
When the Worst Happens and
  You Are a Victim of Fraud 113

Part III

Special Categories Require
Special Strategies

Chapter 11

Buying High-Priced Merchandise Online **119**
Escrow for When a Credit Card Isn't Safe Enough 121
Into Every Great Idea, a Little Fraud Might Fall 121

Chapter 12

Buying Cars Online **125**
Do Your Homework Online 126
Paying for Your Car 128
What to Watch Out For 128
It Goes Both Ways. 129

Chapter 13

Shopping for Real Estate Online. **131**
Finding an Apartment or House to Rent 132
Shopping Online for a Home to Buy 133
Timeshares and Other Vacation Rentals 134

Chapter 14

Buying Travel Services Online 137

Before You Buy 138
Discount Travel Sites Can Mean Big Savings 139
Going Straight to the Source 139
Drawbacks of Internet Travel Shopping 141

Chapter 15

Other Things You Can Buy Online 143

All Kinds of Entertainment 143
The Internet Is a Virtual Drug Store 144
Pet Medications 145
Groceries and Gourmet Foods 146
What's Cooking? 147
Pieces and Parts 147
Gift Giving Online 147
Buying and Selling Gift Cards 149
Online Financial Services 151
Business Supplies 153

Chapter 16

More Than Things: Finding Friends, Dates, and Jobs Online 155

Sharing Common Interests 156
Online Dating 159
Staying Safe in Any Environment 161
Protect Your Pocketbook 163
Looking for Jobs Online 164

Part IV

The Future of Online Shopping

Chapter 17

Looking Ahead 171

Online Shopper's

Appendix

Online Shopping Resources 173
Alphabetical List of Web Sites. 173
List of Web Sites by Categories. 182

Glossary 195

Index 203

Acknowledgments

WHILE I CONSIDER MYSELF TO BE A SAVVY AND KNOW-ledgeable online shopper, this book would have been missing some very valuable information had it not been for the many friends and colleagues who took the time to share their stories and advice.

In particular, I'd like to thank Tracy Anderson; Nancy Burgess (the QVC queen who introduced me to a wonderful new online resource); Suzanne Cloutier; Don and Alice Crow; Charlene Davis; Mark Hamilton and Liz

Ouellette; Christine and Brian Lewis; Ann Marshall (for being smart enough not to become a victim and telling me about it); Candy Morgan; Max Moses; Lynn Pomije; Gene Rooks (my aunt and dear friend); and Jerry & Irene Stoffer (who are both friends and real estate brokers extraordinaire).

I'd also like to express my appreciation to Randy Harden and all the good folks at CarMax who helped with my research and also demonstrated kindness and compassion to our family when my brother-in-law (a CarMax employee) passed away; to Fred Johnson and Tracey Keller, area developers for QuikDrop, who are always willing to help with whatever I need; and Christopher Faulkner, president and founder of CI Host, who shared valuable advice and information.

Of course, this book wouldn't have happened had it not been for the faith and foresight of my editor, Jere Calmes, and all of my wonderful colleagues at Entrepreneur Media Inc.

Finally, I'd like to thank all the online merchants, shoppers, and soon-to-be shoppers who have made this book possible and necessary.

Preface

THE IDEA FOR THIS BOOK WAS CONCEIVED WHEN I WAS IN the middle of researching a book about how to sell on eBay and interviewing a successful eBay seller. Though he was generously sharing tips and advice that would help other sellers, at one point he said, "You know, the book you should really be writing is how to buy online. There are already plenty of online sellers out there. We need more customers."

I mentioned that to my editor, he thought it was a great idea, and here we are.

My goal was to write a book that would include useful advice for the total novice as well as the experienced online shopper. I wanted it to be positive, something that would motivate people to use this incredible resource we call the internet. At the same time, I felt it was necessary to write several lengthy sections on fraud and how to avoid it. As you read those passages, please don't get the idea that the internet is fraught with danger and has criminals lurking around every virtual corner. The reality is that the internet is mostly a positive place, but like any place where humans operate, you'll find good and bad.

Whether you love shopping or consider it a necessary evil (I personally don't care much about the process of shopping; I'm more into acquisitions—shopping is merely the means I must use in order to possess those clever gadgets and other products I find online), you can expand your horizons on the internet. I invite you to join me on an exciting journey into cyberspace.

For Jerry, of course

Part I

Introduction to Online Buying

Chapter 1

How Did We Get Here?

I N THE EARLY DAYS OF ONLINE SHOPPING—WHICH WASN'T so very long ago—it was pretty easy to keep up with all the shopping sites. Today, that would be impossible. There are tens of thousands of online shopping sites, with more being launched daily. The result is an overwhelming range of choices for consumers—choices far beyond what they might be able to find at local retailers, even in shopping meccas such as New York and Los Angeles.

You can find just about anything you might need or want online, from high-end luxury items to groceries. Online stores are open 24 hours a day, 365 days a year. You don't have to get dressed, go out, and find a parking place—you can shop in the comfort of your home, dressed in your jammies (or whatever), with just a computer and a credit card.

Can you get some great deals online? Certainly.

Can you locate hard-to-find items that you thought would be forever elusive? You bet.

Can you save time, money, and energy? Of course.

Can you get ripped off? Most definitely.

But don't stop reading now! The key to successful online shopping is knowledge—knowing how to find what you want, evaluate the seller, and protect yourself. Many of the techniques you'll use are not much different from those you use when shopping in a traditional retail store. What can be both intimidating and exciting is the size and scope of the internet and the consumer opportunities it offers. Before I get into the specifics of how to become a savvy online shopper, I want to look back and show you how the world got to this point.

The More Things Change, the More They Stay the Same

From the time I was a small child, I loved getting mail, not just letters but also packages. I was a dedicated mail order shopper long before I realized what that meant. I grew up and have always lived in suburban areas, so it's not as if I didn't have access to plenty of stores. I just always loved poring over catalogs, fantasizing about owning the merchandise, and perhaps even convincing my mother to buy me a few of those things I just couldn't live without. When I got old enough to make my own purchases, I would carefully fill out the order form, write the check or provide the credit card information, mail it off, then eagerly wait the "four to six weeks" I was asked to "please allow for delivery" until my purchase arrived. Today, I still enjoy browsing through catalogs, but I place my orders online and expect delivery in days, not weeks.

Americans have been able to purchase goods by mail since Colonial times. In fact, ordering from a distance has long been a key element of American and even worldwide commerce. In the 1870s and 1880s, the "modern" mail order industry was born. The early mail order merchants discovered a tremendous market among American farmers and other rural residents who had limited access to retail merchandise, and what was available locally was often expensive.

The country's first mail order business was established in 1872 by Aaron Montgomery Ward. His company's first "catalog" was a single-sheet price list with ordering instructions. By the early 1890s, the Montgomery Ward and Company catalog was 280 pages and advertised some 10,000 items.

Richard W. Sears is credited with establishing the country's most successful mail order house. In 1886, he was working as a railroad station agent and was intrigued both by the high volume of sales literature that was delivered by rail and with the concept that products could be manufactured in one part of the country and sold to customers hundreds, even thousands, of miles away. He began selling watches by mail, sold that business, and in 1894 incorporated Sears, Roebuck and Company in Chicago.

The Sears catalog was sent to thousands of farm homes and emphasized variety, style, and low prices. By 1900, Sears' annual sales reached about $10 million, all through mail order. By 1915, the two industry leaders—Sears and Montgomery Ward—were selling nearly $200 million worth of merchandise annually.

Farmers and small-town residents liked the convenience, selection, and prices offered by mail order companies. In the days before automobiles, a trip to town could take up much of the day, and the offerings of local merchants were limited. Mail order provided access to a wide range of stylish goods and modern conveniences for even the most rural residents.

Automobiles and improved roads contributed to the decline of mail order houses in the 1920s, and many of the previously exclusive mail order operations opened retail stores. The years following World War II saw the advent of a large number of specialty mail-order companies. As more and more women joined the workforce in the second half of the 20th century, they turned to mail order shopping to save time and avoid crowds at stores and malls. Mail order merchants looked for ways to make purchasing easier by offering toll-free telephone ordering and accepting credit cards. And it didn't take those merchants long to see the wisdom of jumping on the e-commerce bandwagon.

Just as they did hundreds of years ago, today's consumers want value, convenience, and choices. And savvy retailers are figuring out better and better ways to give customers what they want.

The Evolution of E-Commerce

Commerce—that is, the buying and selling of goods and services—has existed since the earliest times. In its simplest form, traditional commerce consists of a customer purchasing a product from a supplier. E-commerce is not any different, except that the customer uses electronic signals, usually transmitted over the internet, as the means of making the purchase.

The technology is relatively young. Electronic data interchange (EDI) was standardized in 1984, providing the assurance that companies could reliably complete transactions with one another. The personal computer revolution was just getting underway in the early 1980s, with the introduction of the IBM PC home computer in 1981 and the Apple Lisa and Apple McIntosh computers in 1983 and 1984. The first version of Microsoft Windows was released in 1985. A decade later, two of the biggest names in e-commerce were launched: Amazon and eBay.

Today, an estimated two-thirds of American households have at least one computer, and most of those systems have internet access. As the availability of high-speed internet access continues to rise and the cost continues to fall, people are spending more time—and money—online. It's estimated that by the year 2010, Americans will spend approximately $350 billion online.

Why Shop Online?

What's the appeal of online shopping? As I've mentioned, it's convenient—you do it when you want to, whether that happens to be during traditional operating hours or not. You don't have to drive, you don't have to park, and if an online retailer doesn't have what you're looking for, you can find out with just a few clicks of your mouse instead of a lengthy trek through a store. And for these same reasons, online shopping saves time.

Online shopping allows more time and opportunity for research as well as product and price comparisons. Not sure if you want to buy that specific item from that particular place? If you're online, just bookmark the site (that is, tell your computer to remember it) and come back to it when you've decided.

There's also the issue of privacy. Nobody but you and the supplier know what you're buying online (of course, be sure to check the seller's privacy policy, discussed in the next chapter, to be absolutely certain of that). And in most online transactions, no salesperson is

Shopping Without Driving

Online shopping is a great option for people who may not drive for whatever reason. City dwellers who don't own cars appreciate being able to order online and have their merchandise delivered. People in rural areas with limited access to retailers can easily shop online without having to drive for hours to get to a store and back. Individuals with disabilities that prevent them from driving or just make it difficult to get around, as well as seniors who either have given up driving or just prefer not to do it any more than they have to, appreciate the expanded shopping opportunities available through the internet. My aunt, who is in her 70s, says she just doesn't like to go shopping in stores, so she buys online whenever she can from the comfort of her home. About one-third of the products that she used to purchase in a mall she now buys online.

involved—something many people view as a plus because there's no pressure.

Finally, you can usually find lower prices online than in retail stores—although that's not always the case. (Watch for excessive shipping charges that can inflate the bottom line.) And many shoppers don't mind paying a little extra if that buys them convenience, uniqueness, or another benefit.

Are there drawbacks to shopping online? Sure—a few. You can't see and touch the merchandise—but then, the mail order shoppers of yesteryear couldn't either. In my opinion, the biggest drawback to online shopping is the lack of instant gratification. Of course, if you buy from a retailer that also has a store or other type of local facility, you may be able to pick your purchase up—which gets you the product faster and saves the shipping charges. However, most of the time, you'll have to wait for the item to be shipped to you. If you enjoy getting packages, this will be fun. And you'll likely become good friends with the drivers of the various delivery companies your shippers use.

The exception to lack of instant gratification is when you are purchasing a downloadable digital product—electronic tickets, music, e-books, or other information. Sellers of these items are typically set up so that you can immediately download the digital file as soon as you've paid for it.

Perhaps the most annoying drawback is that e-commerce sites sometimes get overwhelmed during heavy shopping periods, such as major gift-giving holidays (Hanukah, Christmas, Valentine's Day, Mother's Day, etc.), resulting in slower operations and service. Be prepared, and whenever you can, avoid the rush.

Ways to Buy Online

One of the most common ways for people to venture into the online shopping world is to visit the web site of a company they're already doing business with. I began shopping online when my favorite catalogs launched web sites. Then I learned how to use search engines to find products when I didn't have a seller in mind. And then I discovered eBay, and with its wonderful world of things I didn't know I couldn't live without.

Online retailers—or e-tailers—are basically stores that sell to consumers over the internet. Some operate exclusively online; others have brick-and-mortar operations as well. You will also find manufacturers that sell directly to consumers via the internet. Not all manufacturers sell to consumers; many have informative web sites that provide information and details on how you can purchase the products from a retailer or distributor.

When shopping online, you may find yourself in a virtual mall, such as Yahoo! Stores. This is essentially the online equivalent of a brick-and-mortar shopping center, where you can browse around in different stores and compare products and suppliers. There are two basic types of online malls. In one, the various merchants operate independently, just like a mall in the real world. In the other, you actually make all your purchases through the mall instead of from each merchant individually. The latter is easier for the buyer because you don't have to set up a separate account each time you want a different type of product. To find out which type of mall site you're on, click on the Help or About section of the site for information on how it operates.

Then there are the auction sites, such as eBay, where you can buy new and used merchandise from individuals and companies. There are also non-auction online communities where goods similar to those on the auction sites are sold at fixed prices.

Most of the time, the difference won't matter as long as you have located a quality product from a reliable seller. To learn how to do that, let's begin with the basics of online shopping.

Chapter 2

Online Shopping Basics

O GET STARTED SHOPPING ONLINE, ALL YOU NEED IS A computer and modem. I'm going to assume you have those. I'm also going to suggest that if you don't have high-speed internet access that you consider upgrading. I'm not a techie, so I'm not going to recommend any one type of high-speed carrier over another, but trust me when I say this: If you have to wait for web sites to open at dial-up pace, you will find online shopping more frustrating than rewarding. Get the tools you need for the results you want.

Let's start with the basics that apply no matter what you're buying. From a seller's perspective, one of the most important benefits of operating online is that it's a level playing field for suppliers of all sizes. A small homebased company has just as much of a chance of succeeding online as a giant corporation—and it's far easier for that little mom-and-pop business to compete with the big guys online than it is in the brick-and-mortar world. It's often difficult for customers to tell how big a seller is—or isn't. And in this case, size really doesn't matter. What matters is that you get quality products, good service, and competitive prices.

Evaluating an Online Seller

Most people make their initial venture into online shopping by buying from suppliers they have already dealt with in traditional retail stores or by print catalog. That's a pretty safe way to go because you already know the company; you're just completing the transaction in a new way. But what happens when you decide you want something from an online merchant you don't know? Before you place that order, consider the answers to these questions.

How Professional and User-Friendly Is the Web Site?

The better online merchants know to view their sites as their customers do. You should be able to quickly and easily find the information you want about both the company and its products.

With that said, let me add that a poorly-constructed web site does not necessarily mean that you're dealing with a bad company—but you are dealing with a company run by people who don't understand that a user-friendly, informative, easy-to-navigate web site is the first line of top-notch customer service in the e-commerce world. Christopher Faulkner, founder and president of CI Host, a web hosting and data management company, says that an unprofessional web site may be an indicator that the company does not have the resources to build a strong online image, and you need to decide if you want to take your chances with a company that may be very small or strapped for cash.

Faulkner recommends what he calls the ABCs of evaluating a web site:

A stands for About Us. Click on that link and learn what the company is all about—who started it and when, how it has grown, what its policies and procedures are.

B stands for Benefits. Does the site let you know how the company can benefit you? Are the products and market clearly defined? Can you tell why it would be to your advantage to buy from this company over another?

C stands for Choices. Consider the depth of the company's product portfolio. Does it sell just one or two items, or does it have a solid range of products? Do you get the sense that it's a one-hit wonder type of operation or that it's there for the long haul?

Does the Company List a Street Address and Telephone Number as Well as E-Contact Information?

Setting up an online presence is easy and inexpensive—for both legitimate operators as well as scammers. But legitimate companies should tell you where they are located and how to reach them other than through their web sites.

While it's understandable that a homebased business owner may prefer not to list his home address online, you should still look for sufficient off-line contact information to assure you that this is indeed a real company and not an internet scam.

Good contact information is also important from a customer service perspective. A friend of mine who lives in Botswana does a great deal of online shopping and purchased an iPod online. Though the purchase went well, the iPod stopped working after about six months. When she tried to contact Apple through its web site, it was, she says, "a nightmare. I wasted a lot of time trying to figure out how to contact them. The service site is so geared toward having people fix their own problems that it's almost impossible to find the contact information if you can't fix it yourself. It took more than two months to get a useful answer from them." In most cases, you won't need to contact the company offline, but be sure you can if you need to.

Are Products Clearly and Completely Described?

You should be able to get enough information about the merchandise or service to make a sound buying decision. If the description is incomplete or confusing, you may find it difficult to hold the seller responsible if the product is not what you thought or you don't get the service you expected.

What Are the Refund and Return Policies?

No matter how carefully you shop, there will be times when the product just isn't right for whatever reason. Always check the seller's refund and return policy *before* you buy. Be sure the products and your satisfaction are guaranteed. As with brick-and-mortar operations, some online merchants have policies such as store credits instead of cash refunds or restocking fees. I don't like the idea of a store credit; if I return something in resellable condition (or at least in the condition I received it), or if the item is defective, I believe I ought to get my money back, so I don't buy from a company that won't issue a refund. Restocking fees can be reasonable, depending on the product and circumstances—but they shouldn't be a surprise. Find out ahead of time. Be particularly mindful of refund and return policies for customized or personalized items. A merchant might have a more restrictive return policy for items that can't be easily resold.

What Sort of After-Sale Service and Support Does the Company Offer?

The issue of service and support is particularly important when you're buying electronic and mechanical items, but it can apply to just about anything. If you need assistance with set-up, assembly, installation, operation, or whatever, will the company provide it and how will it be delivered (phone, e-mail, online chat, etc.)?

Are There Any Hidden Price Inflators?

You should be able to determine the final price before you provide your credit card information. Be wary of companies that charge excessive amounts for shipping and handling—especially if they're offering bargain prices for their merchandise and compensating for that with disproportionate shipping fees. Always check the shipping before making a final buying decision. A discounted price for the item is worthless if the seller jacks up the shipping to compensate. The same applies to insurance fees; they should be reasonable and in line with the value of the merchandise.

Does the Company Have a Privacy Policy and What Is It?

It's impossible to buy online without providing personal information, but you should know what the company is going to do with that information in addition to processing your order. Some companies make a lot of money selling their customer lists. There's nothing wrong with that—it's a standard business practice that has been used for years in direct mail marketing. But you have the right to know if that's what they're going to do—and if you don't want your information shared or sold, then don't do business with a site that does that.

I prefer to do business with companies that have privacy policies that are sweet and simple—and clear. I have read some privacy policies that are overwhelming in length and complexity, and they make me feel like the company is trying to sneak something past me.

Don't assume that because a company has a link to its privacy policy on the home page that the policy itself is acceptable. The privacy policy may be that the company doesn't share information—or it may be that the company shares its customer list with anybody who wants it. Take the time to read and understand the privacy policy before you decide to do business with a company.

Does the Company Subscribe to Online Consumer Protection Services?

Look for signs such as the SquareTrade (www.squaretrade.com), Web-Assured (www.webassured.com), and other logos that tell you that the company is committed to high service and ethical standards. Remember that these logos can be copied and forged, so click on them to verify that the merchant is truly entitled to use them.

Affiliate Programs

There may be times when you are on one web site and see an ad for or information about a product, and when you click on the link, you are taken to a totally different site. Chances are the web site is participating in an affiliate program, which is an agreement among online advertisers or merchants to pay a commission for referrals or sales. A lot of web site owners make a lot of money through affiliate programs. While that in itself is not an issue to be concerned about, what's important is that you pay attention and recognize if you are routed off the site you intended to visit to one you did not intend to go to. This is not necessarily a bad thing—for example, on my web site I have affiliate links to sites that sell my books—but you always want to know from whom you're buying.

Does the Company Invest in Advertising?

Faulkner says to notice if the company places paid ads in print and online publications or on broadcast outlets. "Most of the time, legitimate merchants will spend money to promote their business," he says. "Scammers or fraudsters won't spend a dime. They put up the web site and hope you stumble upon it, and they can take money from you."

What Do Others Think About the Seller?

Many sites include customer endorsements, and I believe that most of the time those endorsements are legitimate and genuine. But they're not always a reliable indicator of what your experience with that company will be. After all, no company is going to voluntarily post customer complaints on its web site for all to see. But there are ways to check out an online supplier before you buy.

If you can tell where the company is physically located, do a Better Business Bureau search. Go to www.bbb.org and follow the instructions to obtain a BBB reliability report.

A couple of caveats about BBB reports: First, a satisfactory track record with the BBB doesn't necessarily mean that the company is reliable. The majority of online shoppers don't bother to file BBB complaints when they have a problem with an online purchase. If you have a legitimate problem with an online vendor, take the time to file a complaint with the appropriate BBB—your fellow online consumers will appreciate the information, and it might even help you get the situation resolved. Second, an unsatisfactory rating does not necessarily mean you shouldn't do business with the company. The BBB records complaints but does not verify them, so you really have no way of knowing how valid the complaints are. Also, every company is going to have problems, so if you see complaints, consider the overall sales volume of the merchant and keep it in perspective.

You can also do an internet search on the company name and see what comes up. Your search may provide you with links to comment sites, reviews, and even discussion board dialogs about the company.

Check out the various consumer sites that post consumer complaints and comments. Most price comparison sites also offer merchant ratings and product reviews. Keep in mind that any company is going to have some unhappy customers if it has any customers at all, so in addition to checking complaint sites, take the time to review some general business comment sites so you get a complete picture.

Some consumer sites worth looking at include: www.ripoff report.com, www.complaints.com, and www.epubliceye.com. For a fun site full of comments about online and brick-and-mortar companies, check out www.planetfeedback.com.

Always put any negative information you find in context. Remember, companies are operated by humans and humans make mistakes. Even the best of organizations will occasionally drop the ball. And sometimes the problem is not the company's fault but rather unrealistic expectations on the part of the customer. Faulkner says, "Ninety-nine percent of the people on the internet are running a legitimate business and just trying to make money. They want you to return as a customer. They want to save some advertising dollars. So they are going to do a good job for you. They are going to sell the product at a reasonable price, and they are going to take care of you on the service, warranty, and support after the sale." But, he continues, there are some online operators who are "just trying to steal money from people and get a quick dollar." So always do your homework before you make a purchase.

What Do Others Think About the Product?

Whether you make your purchase online or in a brick-and-mortar store, the internet is rich with information and opinions of just about anything you might want to buy. Start by reading the manufacturer's information, then check out the editorial reviews—the reviews written by professional reviewers for publications and industry web sites. Then take a look at

---

Red Flags

As you research sellers, keep these warning signs in mind. They could be clues that the site is bogus or, at the least, the seller isn't always reliable.

- The merchant does not have its own domain name (such as www.mer chantname.com) but rather is using a site set up on a free service such as Geocities or Tripod. You can tell the latter because the name of the free web site service will be included in the web address (example: www.merchantname.tripod.com).

- The web site is poorly designed, difficult to navigate, and includes broken links (that is, links that don't take you anywhere) and images that don't display.

- The merchant does not offer any offline contact information, such as a telephone number or physical address.

- Important customer service details—such as refund and return policies, shipping policies, privacy policies, and after-sale support are not clearly and completely stated.

---

what other consumers who have actually used the product have to say about it. There are a number of sites that allow consumers to post reviews.

When you read consumer reviews, keep in mind that most of these folks are not professional writers, so look beyond the style to the substance. Also, most consumer reviewers are honest and genuinely trying to be helpful—but there are some who just like to post negative reviews about everything they can. So read all the reviews and consider them collectively.

Here are some sites that include consumer reviews:

- *Amazon.com* (www.amazon.com). Though it started as a bookseller, Amazon.com features a wide range of products and allows consumers to review and rank virtually all of them. Whether you buy from Amazon.com or not, it's still worthwhile to check the site for information.
- *ConsumerREVIEW.com* (www.consumerreview.com). Provides reviews and buying advice for outdoor sporting goods and consumer electronics. You can also shop online from this site.
- *Consumer Reports* (www.consumerreports.org). If you like the magazine, you'll love the web site. You can get some information for free, but complete access requires a subscription, which is reasonable and worth the price.
- *ConsumerSearch* (www.consumersearch.com). Gathers and analyzes product reviews and offers a list of top-rated products.
- *Epinions* (www.epinions.com). Offers product reviews and recommendations, plus links to make purchases.
- *Internet Shopper* (www.internetshopper.com). Compares products, prices, and stores.
- *CNET* (www.cnet.com). Offers professional and consumer product reviews and price comparisons for technology-related products; also has free how-to tips for using your electronic devices more efficiently and effectively.

As you read the product description and reviews, look for clues that will tell you if the product is easy to use or assemble, or if it needs extra items (like batteries) to function properly.

Understanding Domain Suffixes

A domain name is the name of a web site. It usually begins with www, then a period (called a "dot" when speaking), then the alphabetic name of the site, then another period, then a suffix that indicates the type of organization that is hosting the site. The suffixes you are most likely to see include:

- *com*. Originally stood for "commercial" to indicate that a site could be used for private, commercial purposes but has evolved to the most well-known top level domain and is used for a wide variety of sites
- *net*. This was first intended for sites related to the internet itself, but now used for a wide variety of sites
- *edu*. Used for educational institutions such as colleges and universities
- *org*. Originally intended for non-commercial organizations, but now used for a wide variety of sites
- *gov*. Used for U.S. government sites
- *mil*. Used for U.S. military sites
- *int*. Used for international sites, usually NATO sites

Domain names may also include a country code that lets you know where the web site is registered. For example, the United Kingdom is .uk, Australia is .au, and Canada is .ca.

The Purchasing Process

Shopping is one thing—buying takes a few more steps. Once you've found what you want, you need to place your order and check out.

I have been on some web sites that seem to make buying the hardest part of the process, but most online sellers have worked hard to develop systems that make it easy for you to make your purchase.

On each product description page, there should be a button labeled "add to shopping cart (or bag or basket)" or "buy now" or something similar. If you have to make choices such as size or color, you will be asked for that either right before or right after you click on the "buy" button. You'll also be asked to enter a quantity. If you forget any of the required information, you'll be reminded before you can continue.

Once the item is in your shopping cart, you'll be asked if you want to check out or continue shopping. Most sites have a button on every page that will allow you to view your shopping cart at any time to see how much you've got in it. On that page, you can make changes to your order, such as increasing quantities, removing items, changing details such as size and color, and so on. I often put everything I see on the site that appeals to me in my shopping cart and then, when I'm ready to actually buy, I review everything I've put in my cart and might delete some things that I've changed my mind about.

When you place an item in your cart, you haven't actually purchased it yet. This is the online equivalent to walking through a physical store, picking things up, and putting them in a real shopping cart. In a physical store, you can decide you don't want some or all of the things you've put in your cart. In that case, you would either put them back on the shelves yourself, give them to the cashier to return to stock when you buy what you do want, or just abandon your cart in the store.

On the "abandon the cart" tactic: in a physical store, that means someone has to put everything back—usually a clerk who probably doesn't think very highly of shoppers who do this. On a web site, you just leave the site without paying, you're not charged for anything, and nobody has to do any work to return to inventory the items you had selected.

Once you have everything you want in your cart and removed anything you don't want, it's time to check out. This is much like the process of checking out at a brick-and-mortar retailer where you take what you want to a cashier who totals your purchases, collects your payment, and bags your purchases.

Online, the checkout process consists of one or more pages where you enter your name, e-mail address, physical address, phone number, shipping instructions, and payment information. You might be asked if

Online Shopper's

you want something else, and you'll have one more chance to review your entire order and see the total amount due, including any taxes and shipping charges. Then you'll be asked to click on a button that says something like "place order now" or "confirm order;" click on this button *once* and wait. It could take several seconds or up to a minute for the

---

If the Site Won't Open

There will be times when for a variety of reasons a particular web site won't open. You'll likely get one of three basic error messages:

1. *Page not found.* The page you're trying to get to either no longer exists or has moved to a new location. Sometimes you'll be automatically forwarded to the new page; other times you'll just be stuck at the error page. Get back to the home page and look for the page you want. For example, if the page has a URL like www.greatshopping.com/ladies-dresses/6up.html, delete everything after the ".com" part and see if you can get to the home page. From there, you can look for the page you want in the index or table of contents. By the way, when I wrote this, the domain name of "www.greatshopping.com" was available for purchase.

2. *Server not found.* It's possible the server may be off-line temporarily because of system maintenance or technical problems, so try again later. If it doesn't work then, chances are the site is just gone. If you really want to find the company, try a general search engine like Google to see if you can find a current web address.

3. *Server connection timed out.* This means your computer couldn't connect with the web site in the time allotted by the server. It could be because too many people were on the site when you tried, or the problem could be somewhere else on the internet. If you're sure the address is good, try again later.

---

site to process your order, and if you click that button more than once, you could create a duplicate order.

Once the order is actually placed and paid for, you'll be taken to a confirmation screen that typically includes an order number and may display the details of your purchase. You'll also get the same information by e-mail. Keep this information either by saving it on your computer or printing it out so that you have all the reference numbers you need if there are any problems with the shipment or other questions later.

Paying for Online Purchases

The best way to pay for online purchases is with a credit card. Period. And it's a great idea to get a credit card that you use exclusively for online shopping so that you can quickly and easily review the charges each month and be sure they match what you actually bought.

Paying by credit card online is fast and safe. Yes, safe. Credit card companies are working hard to protect their customers from fraud. Most cardholder agreements limit your liability for fraudulent charges to $50—and, most credit card companies don't charge you that even though they can. Recently, I got a call from the security department at Discover questioning some online purchases on my account. The charges had been made on Sunday evening; the call came in first thing Monday morning. As it happened, I had made a couple of online catalog purchases on Sunday afternoon, but there were two charges—one to an online auction site I never use and another to an online porn site—that weren't mine (or my husband's, and he has been teased mercilessly by our friends about the porn site charge). Discover immediately closed the account and issued us new cards. It was mildly inconvenient, because we had to take the time to notify the companies that use that account for automatic payments, but we didn't lose any cash.

Another advantage of paying by credit card is that you have additional security because you can dispute the charge if there's a problem, such as if the merchandise doesn't arrive, doesn't work, isn't what you expected, or you returned it and didn't get your refund.

Virtually all online retailers accept credit cards, either as a direct merchant or through an online payment service such as PayPal (more about that shortly). It's a good idea to check to see what payment method the merchant accepts before you spend too much time shopping. Most accept Visa and MasterCard. American Express and Discover charge merchants higher fees than Visa and MasterCard, so some online retailers don't take those cards.

Smaller retailers may not accept credit cards directly but may accept them through online payment services. PayPal, owned by eBay, is probably the best known and most popular online payment service, but there are others, such as BidPay.

Here's how online payment services work: You set up an account with details on how you want to pay (credit card, bank transfer, whatever). When you want to make a payment to a seller that accepts that particular payment service, you just tell the service who to pay. The amount is charged to your credit card or withdrawn from your account and immediately transferred to the seller. If the payment cannot be made electronically, some services will issue a check or money order—this is most commonly used when buying items from individuals overseas.

You could also pay by mailing a check or money order, but there are some drawbacks. First is the convenience factor, especially if you have to go somewhere to purchase the money order. Second is the time it will take to get your merchandise. Many sellers who accept checks and money orders will delay shipping your purchase until your check has cleared or they have been able to confirm the money order is legitimate. Third, and perhaps most important, is that you have no extra layer of consumer protection with checks and money orders as you do when you pay with credit cards. Banks and money order issuers can't do a charge back the way a bankcard merchant account provider can. And finally, while this is not a particularly common issue, the potential for fraud with check payments is higher than with credit cards. Check amounts can be altered, or the seller (or the seller's payment processing staffers) can use the information on your check (your name, address, phone number, and bank account number) to steal from you later.

Most online merchants do not accept cash—and you shouldn't pay with cash anyway. Cash is easily lost or stolen, and you have no way of proving how much you sent if the total doesn't arrive. Reserve paying cash for face-to-face transactions.

Another online payment option that is more commonly used with high-dollar purchases is an escrow service. This is where you deposit the funds with an independent third party. The merchant ships when it receives confirmation that the funds have been deposited. When you receive the merchandise and advise the escrow company that you are satisfied, the funds are released to the seller. If you are not satisfied or you don't receive the goods, the funds are held while you resolve the problem with the merchant.

Don't use a debit card for online purchases. While most online payments are processed without a problem, if yours happens to be the exception, using a debit card could give a hacker or scammer access to your entire bank account. While debit cards do offer some security and fraud reimbursement programs, most debit cards do not offer the same level of protection that is available with a credit card.

Do You Have to Pay Sales Tax?

Sales tax on internet purchases is a sticky issue. The general rule is that if you and the online merchant are in the same state, you'll pay sales tax based on your state's laws. If the online merchant is located in another state but has a physical location in your state, you pay sales tax. But if the online merchant is located in another state and does not have an operation in your state, you probably won't pay sales tax.

When my husband was shopping for a digital camera, he found what he wanted at a good price at www.costco.com (Costco Wholesale's online store). He also found the same camera for slightly more at a store that sells online and has a retail location in New York. We're in Florida, and Costco has warehouse stores here. We would have had to pay Florida state sales tax on the Costco purchase, but the New York seller didn't charge sales tax. The bottom line was that even though Costco's price was lower, the total was higher because of the sales tax. Both merchants give excellent service, so the deal really came down to price, and the sales tax made the difference.

Brick-and-mortar stores have been crying "unfair" about this for a long time and periodically legislation is proposed that would force all online merchants to collect and remit the sales tax charge to the state in which their customers are located. That would be a tremendous administrative burden for smaller operations, and so far such measures have failed. But things could change at any time.

When Will You Get Your Order?

Most online merchants ship within a day or two of receiving your order. Most also will give you a choice of shipping methods—standard or various levels of expedited—and you can decide which you want based on when you need the merchandise and the cost.

An increasing number of online merchants follow up the order confirmation e-mail with a shipping confirmation e-mail. This tells you what carrier was used and gives you a tracking number so you can monitor the progress of the shipment. Some merchants have links on their sites that will let you check the status of your order.

Typical online purchases take anywhere from a few days to a few weeks to arrive. A friend of mine recently bought an iPod that was shipped from China and arrived in Florida in three days. Even ground shipments within the United States rarely take more than a week in transit. As a customer service measure, the seller should let you know when your order has been shipped.

The Federal Trade Commission's rules for mail and telephone orders also apply to orders placed online. That means that sellers should state when products will be shipped, and if they don't, they must ship within 30 days of receiving the order. If there's a delay for any reason, they must notify you, provide a revised shipment date, and give you the option to cancel and get a full and prompt refund. In fact, many online retailers don't charge your credit card until your order is shipped, but they still must comply with the deadlines and notification requirements. Most online retailers know the rules and are set up to abide by them.

It's not uncommon for items featured on web sites to be back-ordered—that is, the merchant doesn't have the item in stock, but you can go ahead and place your order, and it will be shipped when it's available. Many merchants are set up for you to be notified of backorder status when you put the item in your shopping cart; others will notify you in a follow-up e-mail or via snail mail.

If you have to provide a signature for the package when it arrives, check the exterior for signs of damage before you sign off on it. If the package is crushed, torn, or looks like it's been opened and retaped, make a note to that effect when you sign. Whether you sign for the shipment or it was left at your door, immediately open it and confirm that your order is complete and in good condition. Compare the packing slip to the contents and keep in mind that it's possible items could arrive separately.

It Arrived and Something's Wrong

Most online transactions go smoothly, but occasionally you'll have a problem. The item could be damaged in transit, the seller may have made a mistake filling your order, the product may be defective, or a host of other possibilities. When there's a problem, your first step is to contact the seller either by phone (they should provide a toll-free number) or e-mail. Be polite, concise, and complete; explain what the problem is and ask for instructions on how to proceed. See Chapters 9 and 10 for common problems and how to deal with them.

Was the Shipment Insured?

When you buy from most online companies, the seller is responsible for the item until it's in your hands. That means if you don't receive the package for any reason—for example, if it was lost by the shipper or even stolen off your front porch—or it was damaged in transit, the seller must either replace the merchandise or issue a refund. Under those circumstances, it's up to the seller to purchase insurance from the carrier. Some carriers provide a minimum amount of coverage automatically, and high-volume sellers typically self-insure for any amount above that

Online Shopper's

The QVC Queen

When I was asking people for their online shopping stories as research for this book, I got one that surprised me. Nancy Burgess told me that she was the "QVC Queen." You may know that QVC is a 24-hour television shopping network. It also has a web site (www.qvc.com) where you can purchase the items shown on TV and more. Nancy says, "They sell everything from clothes to food to household products, and I've tried some of everything."

Though she sometimes watches the television programming, she rarely buys from that. Instead, if she sees something of interest, she makes a note of the product and goes online later to make the purchase. She praises QVC's service and the quality. In one situation, she sent a gift of crab cakes to a friend, not knowing that the friend would be out of town. The package was left on the doorstep and, of course, spoiled. Nancy e-mailed QVC, and the shipment was replaced. Her advice for online shoppers: "Try one or two products from a web site and if neither are what you're looking for, don't make any further purchases from that site."

maximum meaning that they set aside funds to cover losses and do not purchase insurance.

The exception is when you are buying through online auctions, particularly from individuals and small companies. Often those sellers will make insurance optional but state that if you refuse it, the seller is not responsible for nondelivery or damage.

Money-Saving Tips

Shopping online is the easiest way to find the lowest price for whatever it is you want. But there are plenty of ways to save money besides just getting a good buy.

- *Sales, specials, and closeouts.* Just like brick-and-mortar stores, online retailers often have sales and reduce items to clear out their inventories. Check your favorite sites regularly, or sign up for e-mail alerts.

- *Manufacturer rebates.* Rebates are not limited to traditional retail transactions—you can get them with online purchases as well. To find out what rebates are being offered by which manufacturers, visit a rebate-tracking site, such as www.myrebates.com or www.rebateshq.com. But if you find a rebate and use that in your decision-making process, be sure to follow up and file the necessary forms to get your money. Manufacturers know many of their customers won't bother.

- *Online coupons.* Online coupons work the same way paper coupons do, except that instead of handing a cashier a slip of paper, you enter a code during the checkout process. Many merchants issue online coupons for various types of discounts; you'll

Online Coupon Sources

The following sites are great sources for finding promotional codes and special offers that can save you big bucks:

www.ableshoppers.com

www.coolsavings.com

www.couponcabin.com

www.couponmountain.com

www.currentcodes.com

www.dealcatcher.com

www.dealhunting.com

www.dealtaker.com

www.fatwallet.com

www.hotdealsclub.com

www.shoppersresource.com

find them in catalogs, direct mail pieces, and even in the inserts with your order (a way to get you to buy again). You can also find coupons at web sites designed to help you save money. My friend Brian Lewis offers this advice, "Shop and find the best deal on what you want, then go looking for a coupon to bring the price down even further." An interesting note is that Brian says he feels cheap when he uses a coupon in a brick-and-mortar store but not when he's buying online.

- *First-time customer discounts and specials.* Many e-tailers offer special deals to customers making their first purchase. Those deals might be a discount of a flat amount or a percentage on that purchase, a coupon for discounts on future purchases, free shipping, a free gift, free gift-wrapping, or whatever. If you're making your first purchase from a particular merchant, check around the site to see what sort of bonuses are available.

- *Free or reduced shipping.* In general, the buyer pays the shipping for online purchases, but merchants often offer specials on their shipping rates just as they do on their products. An increasing number of merchants are offering free shipping, or free shipping with purchases over a certain amount. A site I buy from occasionally offers special shipping deal of 99 cents during a specified period, no matter how much you order. A friend of mine orders regularly from a few sites that periodically offer free shipping; she waits to make all of her purchases from those sites for the time when she won't have to pay shipping.

- *Have your entire order shipped together.* If you're buying more than one item from a site, it's possible things will be available at different times. Some sites charge the same total amount for shipping regardless of when various items go out, but some sites charge more if they have to make separate shipments. In those cases, requesting that everything in your order be shipped together can save you money. Also, if you're not in a rush and the site offers shipping choices, choose the slowest—it's usually the cheapest.

- *Get on merchants' mailing lists.* Many merchants will ask if you'd like to be on their mailing lists. If this is a company you expect to buy from again, say yes. You'll get notices of special sales, clearance items, coupons, and other special offers.

Sometimes Brick-and-Mortar Is Best

There will always be times when an e-tailer just can't do the job because you need face-to-face contact. For example, my husband and I are runners, and we prefer to buy our running shoes from a local store rather than online. The staff is comprised of knowledgeable runners, and when they can see our old shoes to check the wear patterns, watch us move, and listen to our comments, they can make good suggestions for the right kind of shoe. Then we can try on several different styles before making a decision. You can't get that kind of service online. A friend of ours—also a runner—puts it this way, "Sometimes I just need a brick-and-mortar experience."

Of course, once you've found something that works for you, you can switch to an online supplier to save time and money. But always be fair to the local retailers. Don't take their time doing your research if you have no intention of buying from them.

Chapter 3

From Teenagers to Seniors: Generational Issues

ONE OF THE MOST EXCITING THINGS ABOUT THE INTERNET in general and online shopping in particular is that there are virtually no age limits in either direction. If you can operate a keyboard, you can shop online, no matter how old, young, or young-at-heart you happen to be.

Young People

Today's youngsters are totally comfortable doing all kinds of things online, and if they have access to credit cards, they can do some serious shopping—and equally serious financial damage and perhaps even put themselves in danger—with or without your permission. So how do you make sure your kids practice safe online shopping habits?

Most important, know what they're doing online. Don't just give them computers and modems and let them go browsing. Use the internet with your kids, learn about the technology together, and simply accept the fact that it is likely that your kids will have a better understanding of technology than you. Christopher Faulkner says he thinks most kids know more than their parents about the internet, so show interest and let them teach you. In the process, set limits on what they can do online. "Turn off the computer, sit down with the kids, and lay down some ground rules," Faulkner advises.

Be sure your kids know never to give any personal information to people they meet online. And be careful that you don't inadvertently do the same. If, for example, you have a family web site with your children's pictures, don't include details like where they go to school, your phone number or address, or any other information that could identify your kids and possibly put your family at risk. Your children should know to never plan a face-to-face meeting with someone they have met online, and they should notify you if they are approached for such an offline meeting.

Establish clear rules for using the internet for shopping and other purposes. Learn about the various parental control tools, protective software, and controlled access options that are available so you can decide which, if any, are best for you and your family.

Keep in mind that your kids could be a great online shopping resource for you. A youngster who enjoys surfing the 'net may be happy to do mom and dad a favor by gathering product and purchase information for you.

Also keep in mind that youngsters tend to be very trusting and gullible. They generally see all adults as authority figures and believe what they're told, so before you purchase something on their recommendation, check it out for yourself.

Seniors

An increasing number of seniors are getting online. Many are content with just using their computers for e-mail and photo sharing, but others have recognized the value of online shopping. Like youngsters, seniors are sometimes more vulnerable to unscrupulous sellers and online scams. Many grew up in a time and place where everybody knew everybody else, people didn't lock their doors, and local merchants were committed to customer satisfaction.

If you are a senior venturing into the world of online shopping, be very cautious and skeptical. Start by shopping with merchants that you already have a relationship with. Take the time to research and evaluate e-tailers before you buy. Never respond to an unsolicited e-mail offer of any kind—if you have not given that seller permission to e-mail you, delete the message without opening it. Don't let a scammer trick you or intimidate you into making a purchase you don't want, giving out personal information, or participating in or being the victim of a fraud. Be skeptical of everything until you have enough evidence to trust that the deal is good.

Age Doesn't Matter

The bottom line on the issue of age and internet shopping is that age doesn't matter. It's human nature to want to trust people, to want to get a good deal, and to want to take advantage of opportunities when they come your way. But people of all ages are getting ripped off on the internet every day—and in most cases, it happens because they didn't do their homework and follow the advice of experts on how to avoid being a victim.

Chapters 9 and 10 discuss consumer protection issues and frauds and scams in great detail. Everyone, no matter how young or old, should read those chapters carefully. Be sure you understand the advice before you get online. Faulkner says, "There is nothing worse than getting ripped off. You feel like you are a total idiot when it happens to you." So be smart and don't let it happen.

Part II

Let's Go Shopping

Chapter 4

Online Auctions

ONE OF THE MOST POPULAR WAYS TO BUY ONLINE IS through auctions. People have sold goods by auctions for thousands of years, and it's only logical that the auction process has evolved and improved over the years. Auctions found their way onto the internet in the mid-1990s, and today you can buy just about anything on online auction sites.

The largest and most well-known online auction site is eBay. It began in 1995 as a simple little web site created to provide buyers and sellers with a cyberplace where they could trade directly with one another. In the following decade, eBay grew to a massive international operation with millions of users buying and selling new and used goods and services in both auction and online store formats. Even people who aren't sure what it is have heard of eBay with its whimsical logo, clever ads, and phenomenal growth.

But eBay is not the only auction game in town. Online auctions are a multibillion-dollar industry (yes, that's billion with a B). There are hundreds of auction sites operating around the world. Some are general sites trying to compete with eBay; others specialize and restrict listings to a particular category, such as art, automobiles, books, electronics, memorabilia, business services, travel, and so on. You might want to check out these sites: www.bidville.com, http://auctions.shopping .yahoo.com (Yahoo!'s auction site), and http://auctions.overstock.com (Overstock.com's auction site).

What's most important to remember when you are shopping on an auction site is that you are not buying from the site. The site is simply providing an electronic venue for the buyer and seller to reach an agreement. A friend of mine had a bad experience with her first eBay transaction: She won the auction and paid, but the seller never shipped the product and did not respond to follow-up e-mails. That was several years ago, and my friend still refuses to shop on eBay. Even though she understands intellectually that the problem was not with eBay but with that particular seller, she still thinks of eBay as a place where she got ripped off.

Among the thousands of consumer fraud complaints received every year by the Federal Trade Commission (FTC), those dealing with online auction fraud consistently rank at or near the top of the list. The complaints generally involve products that are shipped late or not at all, products that are not of the same quality as advertised, bogus online payment or escrow services, and fraudulent dealers who lure bidders off the legitimate auction sites with seemingly better deals. It's not uncommon for the problem to be unintentional—that is, sometimes the sellers are inexperienced and make mistakes that escalate into serious situations. Of course, while you might have a certain amount of understanding for an inexperienced seller who made a mistake in a description or didn't realize how important prompt shipping is, you're still a customer who wants—and is entitled to receive—what you were promised. It's also worth noting that while most online auction complaints are against the sellers, there are times when the buyers are the problem.

With that said, online auctions are still a relatively safe, efficient, and fun way to shop. I have purchased hundreds of items on eBay without any problems and routinely check eBay first whenever I'm shopping for something—even when I'm not entirely sure what I'm looking for. Not long ago, I found a recipe for cream cheese mints that sounded easy and yummy. But the recipe called for mixing up the ingredients and then using a "super shooter" to form the mints. I'm a reasonably adequate cook and know how to use a variety of kitchen utensils, but I had no idea what a "super shooter" was. So I did a search on eBay and quickly found out that it's a handy little electric or battery-operated gadget for making cookies and decorating food, and a bunch of them were up for sale on eBay for bargain prices. I was happy to get a used unit at less than half of what it would have sold for new.

Online auctions are also a great way to find parts of sets as well as old stuff—not necessarily antiques. A friend of mine says she finds "things you can't find anywhere else—like the lid to a 1950s cookie jar or the hard-to-find gravy boat that matches your china pattern but isn't sold anywhere else at a reasonable price." I had a three-piece set of PartyLite candleholders and one broke when I dropped it (as glass will do with it connects abruptly with a tile floor). It had been long enough since I had bought the set that I didn't have the contact information for the distributor. Also, this wasn't the first time I'd broken (and then replaced) one of the pieces in this set, so I had an idea of the cost to do that as a new retail purchase. I did an eBay search—and thousands of PartyLite items popped up. I was able to find the entire set used for slightly less than it would have cost to replace just the broken piece through a distributor.

When it comes to old but not ancient items, eBay can be a fabulous resource. Traditional retailers naturally focus on the latest and greatest and most up-to-date products—but what if that's not what you want? What if last year's technology is all you need? What if a style of two or three seasons ago suits you perfectly? You can find these items at bargain prices on eBay and other online auction sites. When a friend of mine learned how to use a particular piece of software at work and then quit her job, she wanted to have that program on her computer at home. But the software company had upgraded it and she really didn't want to learn the new edition. She wanted what she was familiar with, and it wasn't available in retail stores. She searched eBay and found a new, shrink-wrapped edition of the version she wanted that was several years old. The software originally sold for about $300; she got it for $5.

People who always want to have the latest in gadgets often sell their used items—which may be relatively new and are usually in great condition—on online auctions. Here's one more story, and then we'll move on to the nuts and bolts of auction shopping. I have a small MP3 player that I clip to my waist when I run so I can listen to music. After about a year and a half, the on/off switch on my first player wasn't working right. I figured it was probably because of the perspiration (okay, sweat) that I got on the player every time I used it. I wanted to replace the old player, but I didn't want to have to learn to use something different (either the player or the software that loads the music onto it), and I didn't particularly want to pay retail for something that I was probably going to ruin in 18 months. So I went on eBay and found the exact player that I had for sale by someone who had bought a new iPod and didn't need the old player anymore. I got it for about 20 percent of the new cost and didn't have to take the time to learn how to use it. My point is this: Whenever you want something that is slightly out of date, whether new or used, check auction sites first.

How Online Auctions Work

You probably have a pretty good idea of how real-world auctions work. People gather in a room, the auctioneer holds up the item, and bidders shout out what they're willing to pay. The person willing to pay the most—the highest bidder—wins the right (and obligation) to purchase the item.

Online auctions work in much the same way. A seller puts an item up for auction with a minimum, or starting, bid amount. People place competing bids until the item is ultimately sold to the highest bidder. The big difference between real-world and online auctions is that in a live auction, the item stays on the auction block until the bidding stops—the old "going once, going twice, sold to the man in the black hat" sort of thing. Typically online auctions are up for a specific time period, generally anywhere from one to ten days, and when the time is up, the highest bidder wins. If, for example, you place the highest bid on the second day of a five-day auction, you have to wait until the auction closes to claim your item.

Most of the online auction sites also offer sellers the option of listing their items for a fixed price, which takes the bidding element out of the transaction. For the buyer, it means that you don't have to wait until the end of the auction to see if you are the high bidder and are going to get to buy the item.

Before you start doing any serious shopping at any auction site, allow a few hours to browse around the site and get comfortable with how it works and what the policies and procedures are.

Just as you would have to register and check in at a live auction, you must first register to bid or buy on any online auction site. This protects everybody from fraud and other problems. On eBay, for example, you just go to www.ebay.com, look for the box that says "Welcome New Users," click on "Register Now," and follow the simple steps. Other auction sites have similar registration procedures.

Finding What You Want

Most auction sites are segregated by categories—eBay, for example, has thousands of categories. While some people will browse through categories looking for something that might catch their eye, most shoppers search by keywords because they know that sellers are often unpredictable when choosing what categories they're going to list their products in.

The auction sites have a search box on their home page, and typically offer you the option of doing a basic search or an advanced search, which lets you add parameters beyond the basic item name. I'll use eBay as an example, but keep in mind that the process is very similar on all auction sites.

Say that you like the clothing and accessories sold by Chico's. You can type "Chico's" in the search box, and you'll get literally thousands of results—items with "Chico's" in the title that could be new or used, clothing or accessories, any size, any color, and probably a few listings that have nothing to do with the Chico's clothing chain. You can narrow the results by being more specific; type "Chico's belt" in the search box, and you'll get a far shorter list of results. Add another descriptive word—maybe a color or fabric—and you'll narrow it down even more. You can streamline your search further by using the advanced search features that allow you to enter additional information such as price range, location, exclusions, payment methods, or other specifics.

If you want two or more words searched in a specific order, place quotations around the phrase (for example, "Chico's pants"). However, if the seller hasn't used that exact phrase in the title (for example, the seller's title is "Chico's black gaucho style pants"), this approach can eliminate many auctions you might want to see. Whenever you're looking for something you haven't searched for before, experiment with several keyword combinations to see what gives you the best results.

By default, eBay conducts keyword searches on auction titles only. You can get more results by checking the "search title and description" box below the keyword box. You may be surprised at how often the keyword you're searching on isn't in a title but appears in the description because the seller thought other words were more appropriate or important to include in the limited space of the title. For example, you may be searching for a ladies' white gold and diamond watch. The seller could title the auction "New Ladies' Designer Watch" and in the body of the description mention that the watch is white gold and has diamonds around the face. If you search on titles only, you'll miss this listing.

Another way to broaden your search is to use a "wildcard" or asterisk (*) after a keyword. For example, if you search for *possum**, your results will include listings with the words: opossum, o'possum, possums or possum's. Once you have that broad list, you can streamline your search by adding other criteria or excluding certain words from that search.

You can also used the wildcard to eliminate specific groups of words from your search. For example, if you're looking for a list of Craftsman products other than tools, put a minus sign in front of the word "tool" and an asterisk after it, like this: *Craftsman-tool**. Your results will exclude Craftsman products with the whole or partial word tool in the name, such as tools, toolbox, toolbag, toolset, toolkit, etc.

Unless you specify a category when you conduct a keyword search, your results will list items from all over the eBay world. For instance, if you typed "white oleander" in the search box the results would include movies, books, soundtracks, and shrubs. But if you are just looking for the film by that title on DVD, select the DVD category before conducting your search. Narrow your search even further by specifying "new" or "factory sealed" DVDs.

The Seller Might Have Something Else You Want

All auction descriptions give you the option to "view seller's other items" by clicking on a link in the "Seller Information" box. When your keyword search brings up something you're looking for, you may find that seller has similar or additional items that you might also be interested in. If you buy more than one item from a particular seller and everything can be shipped together, your shipping costs will naturally be less than if each item shipped separately. Most sellers pass this savings along to their customers; in eBay language, sellers say they will "combine shipping" on multiple purchases. It's a win-win deal because you save money on shipping and the seller makes an additional sale.

Once you know a seller, you can routinely search on his User ID to see what he's offering, or you can visit his eBay store if he has one. Do this with the Refine or Advanced Search feature. eBay does not provide

Online Shopper's

a search tool once you are in the list of a particular seller's current listings; however, you can use the Ctrl-F function (search in top window) to find items by keywords.

Misspellings Can Spell B-A-R-G-A-I-N-S

Bargains on online auctions often come in the guise of misspellings—and you can use these mistakes to your advantage. Remember, the majority of auction shoppers search by keyword rather than category, so when a seller makes a mistake in the spelling of the item's name, the listing won't be easy to find. And the items not being viewed and bid on by others are likely to sell at a bargain price to one of the few shoppers savvy enough to find them.

The best way to search for misspellings is to think about different mistakes a seller might make when writing the title or description for their items. Then type those misspelled words into the search box, and see what kind of results you get. Let's say you're looking for candles or candleholders; if the seller typed "candels," many people shopping for candles would overlook the listing, and it's possible the closing bid could be a fraction of the item's true value. This is a great technique for all kinds of items, but especially for collectibles.

You can also use a wildcard of asterisk (*) to find misspellings in auction titles. You could search for typos such as "cand*" and you'll get listings for any word that begins with those four letters. That's a pretty generic thing, but consider how you might apply it to the particular items you want to buy. You'll figure out plenty of creative ways to discover bargains hidden by misspelled words. Develop a special search list that you use on a regular basis specifically for these typos.

Imitation Is the Highest Form of Flattery

Watch other bidders and copy their techniques. It's called shadowing, and it's another way to find some good bargains that may be flying under the radar. On every auction description page on eBay, the history shows how many bidders have bid on that item to date. Click on that link to see a list of all the bidders (which is available except when the auction is private; in that case, only the seller knows who the bidders are). To decide who to shadow, choose either the high bidder or a bidder with a relatively high feedback number, which indicates he is an experienced eBayer. Make a note of his User ID and go to an advanced search page (which can be accessed from almost any eBay page) and click the "Find items by bidder" link. Enter a User ID, and decide if you want to see all of the current auctions the bidder is interested in or just the ones she is the high bidder on. You can also look at closed auctions he has bid on.

This search will pull up a list of auctions, some of which may be of interest to you. As you look at those listings, note which ones escaped your notice during your own search query and figure out why. Was it something in the title or description? Perhaps a misspelled word or extra detail you didn't include in your search criteria?

Keep in mind that the flip side to shadowing bidders is that someone may want to shadow you. To keep others from seeing what items you're interested in, which potentially draws attention to that auction and could raise the bid, don't place a bid until the near the close of the auction. Use the "Watch this item" link to make it easy to monitor the auction.

Don't Re-Create the Wheel

Once you have a search defined exactly the way you want it, save it by clicking on the "Add to Favorites" link on eBay (or whatever save command other auction sites use). That specific search will be filed in your "My eBay" section. You can either check it on your own schedule or have eBay send you an e-mail notification when new auctions that match your parameters have been posted.

You can also save your Favorite Categories, Favorite Sellers, and Favorite Stores, and store them in My eBay. By doing this, whenever you want to access one of your favorites, you can either go to My eBay or use the "Shortcuts to My Favorites" drop-down menu found on the bottom of most eBay pages.

Of course, you can simply bookmark a search page and save it on your computer. But when you use this method, eBay cannot help you keep track of your favorites.

Do You Know from Whom You're Buying?

A common question asked by people who have never shopped on eBay is, "How do I know I'm dealing with someone who is reputable?" Each eBay listing includes a "Seller Information" box that will show you the seller's status with eBay and allow you to see what other people have to say about the seller. The box also has links so you can ask the seller a question, view other items the seller has posted, or visit the seller's eBay store if she has one.

A key part of the seller information box is the feedback section. eBay's feedback system allows every buyer and seller to post a comment about every completed transaction. The comments can be categorized as positive, neutral, or negative, and eBay automatically calculates a feedback score based on a point system. After a seller's User ID, you'll see a number in parentheses; this is the feedback score, which is the number of eBay members that are satisfied doing business with a particular member. In the Seller Information box, you'll see a positive feedback percentage. This is essentially the satisfied customer ratio; it is calculated by dividing the number of members who have left positive feedback by the

---

Know Your Seller

Before you bid on an item or make a fixed-price purchase from an eBay seller you haven't bought from before, review the data in the Seller Information box.

---

number of members who have left both positive and negative feedback. Generally a feedback percentage of 98 or higher is acceptable, although you might consider buying from a seller with a lower percentage if you check him out carefully. Because this is a percentage figure, remember that the feedback percentage of a relatively new seller with just a few transactions can be seriously skewed by one negative post. Also, when considering the feedback rating, pay attention to whether the feedback applies to purchases or sales—if most of the feedback is in response to the user's buying activities, you can't tell much about his integrity as a seller.

When the positive feedback percentage is anything less than 100, check to see when the negative feedback was posted (if it was a long time ago, the seller may have made some mistakes and mended his ways; if it was recent, it could be a red flag), exactly what was said, and if the seller posted a response. You should be able to tell if this was a simple misunderstanding, an honest mistake, or an intentional attempt to cheat someone.

Most of the major online auction sites have similar feedback systems. Take the time to figure out how each one works so you can evaluate sellers before you bid.

Another important piece of information in this box is how long the seller has been an eBay member. Certainly everybody has to be new at first, but be cautious when making purchases from someone who is new, or relatively new, even if they have a positive feedback score.

An eBay seller I know sold an inexpensive downloadable digital product (an e-book) to a guy who, within hours of the sale, began pestering her to leave him feedback. My friend is very efficient and uses a system of leaving all her feedback at once, one time each day. By the time she was ready to leave feedback on this particular transaction, the buyer had already sent her several e-mails demanding that she leave positive feedback for him. Because he had paid promptly, she did leave positive feedback, but in her remarks noted that he had been pushy about it. At that point, his feedback rating indicated that he had ten completed transactions—all purchases. When he read her comment, he

Online Shopper's

blasted her with a rude e-mail. A few days later, just out of curiosity, she checked his feedback status and it was up to 60—more purchases of similar inexpensive downloadable digital products. A week or so later, she noticed that he had put up some items for sale—computers and other electronics—and in his description, stressed his "high positive feedback rating" as a reason buyers could feel safe doing business with him. He had clearly manipulated the system to achieve that high feedback rating, and an inexperienced eBay shopper wouldn't realize it. Was there anything wrong with the electronics he was selling? I don't know, but his behavior was certainly suspicious.

Tracey Keller, an area developer with QuikDrop, a franchise of stores that will sell items for you on eBay, is also an avid eBay shopper. She says she will rarely buy from someone unless they have at least 50 feedback reports, with half of them being from buyers. "Someone could have 200 feedbacks, but they could all be from buying, so you don't know if they are a good and trustworthy seller," she says.

Can You Get a Good Look?

In the traditional retail world, you can see and touch things before you buy. In the online auction world, you have to depend on written descriptions and photographs. Many eBay buyers refuse to even look at an item that doesn't include a picture; my advice is to be careful about bidding on or buying items without a picture. But, remember, if the item doesn't have a picture, the number of potential bidders is reduced, and that means you could get a bargain. But you need to be sure you know what you're bidding on.

A picture is the best way to know that the seller actually has what he's selling. It's also the best way for you to be sure the item is what is being described. If the listing doesn't include a picture and it's something you're interested in, ask the seller to send you one.

Look carefully at each photograph the seller has posted. Does it match the description? Does it appear to be blurry or doctored? Check some of the seller's current and previous auctions to see if the photo is a duplicate of similar auctions they have posted. If so, you may not be looking at an actual picture of the item up for sale. Some sellers will lift photos from other auctions, web sites, and even print catalogs. Though this is usually a copyright violation, it's often done more due to laziness and ignorance than dishonesty.

If you have any doubts or questions about what you see in the photo, ask the seller for clarification or a picture of the item at a different angle. If the seller is using a digital camera, this shouldn't be a problem. And the manner and time in which they reply will give you more insight to their reliability.

You've Searched, You've Found It, You Want It—What Now?

Once you find an item you want, you're ready to bid—right? Wrong. There are a few things you should do before placing a bid.

You need to decide how much you're willing to pay for the item, and to do that, you need to know what it's worth. If it's a new item, find out what you could buy it for in a store or from another online source. If it's used or refurbished, the value will be less than new, and you can probably estimate it based on the value of what it sold for new and its current condition. Once you know its value, you can let that guide you in determining your top bid.

Take the time to read the entire auction description carefully. Pay attention to the seller's terms and conditions, and be sure they're acceptable to you. For example, some sellers will only accept certain payment methods; some will only ship to certain areas; some require that a new bidder with minimal feedback contact them before bidding.

Check out the kind of guarantee the seller offers. What is the return policy? It's understandable when used items are sold "as is," but an "all sales are final, no exceptions" policy could be a red flag about the quality of merchandise or the type of customer service the seller provides. If the seller has a "no returns, no refunds" policy, are you willing to take the risk of not being happy with your purchase? It's a judgment call—if the seller has strong positive feedback and you can get the item for a good price, it might be worth the chance.

Many sellers, especially new or occasional ones, don't include return or refund policy information in their listings. You may want to send them an e-mail before you bid and ask for those details. Most sellers will allow you to return an item for a refund of the purchase price (but not shipping charges) if you are dissatisfied.

If you have any questions about the item or the terms, ask before bidding. If a picture was not provided or if it's fuzzy, e-mail the seller to request a clear photo. If the description does not provide enough details, ask for more.

If delivery time is important, find out in advance what the approximate delivery date will be. You can usually determine this by the type of shipping the seller uses, and how soon after the close of the auction they will ship. Most sellers will state their shipping procedures in the auction description or on their "About Me" page, but if you can't find that information, ask.

Once you know what you're bidding on, are comfortable with the seller and the seller's terms, and have decided what the item is worth to you, it's time to get in the game.

Do I Hear a Dollar?

The bidding process on eBay is simple: Just click on "place bid," and follow the prompts. It's similar on other online auctions. Always keep in mind that while auction shopping may be fun, it's not a game—your bid is a legal contract, a commitment to purchase the item at the specified price if you are the winner of the auction. Don't bid unless you're serious about buying.

There are a few circumstances when a bid can be retracted. If you make an error when entering your bid—for example, you meant to bid $5.00 and accidentally typed $50.00—you may retract that bid, but you must immediately re-enter the correct amount. If the description of an item changes substantially after you've bid on it, you may retract your bid. You may also retract a bid if you have tried unsuccessfully to reach the seller by phone or e-mail. And, of course, if someone else places a bid using your User ID (which is fraud), that bid can be retracted.

Some bidders will decide they don't want an item after winning an auction and simply don't pay for it. This is a violation of the contract you agreed to when you placed your bid, and it's also a violation of eBay's policies. Not paying for auctions you have won can earn you the status of "nonpaying bidder" and get you kicked off the auction site.

There are two ways to bid on eBay. You can manually place each bid as the auction progresses, or you can use eBay's automatic system known as proxy bidding.

If you were at a traditional auction, you would call out your bids to the auctioneer until you either reached your maximum amount or until everyone else stopped bidding and you won the auction. That's essentially what you would be doing by manually bidding on eBay.

But let's say you couldn't go to a particular auction and there was something there you wanted. So you ask a friend—a proxy—to go and bid on your behalf. You tell the proxy what your maximum bid is, and the proxy would place incremental bids until either winning the auction or until the bids exceeded your limit.

eBay's system works much the same way. When you place your bid, you can enter the maximum amount you're willing to pay. The system places bids on your behalf, bidding only as much as is necessary to maintain your position as the high bidder until it reaches your maximum amount.

Whether you are bidding manually or using the proxy system, eBay will notify you by e-mail if you are outbid. At that point, you can decide if you want to increase your bid or let the item go. This is the time when you are at greatest risk of catching auction fever, which could spark a bidding war that will drive the final price up far past the item's true value.

Catching auction fever means losing control in the bidding process and bidding far more than you can afford or than the item is worth. You can avoid this by knowing the value of what you're bidding on, setting a maximum bid before you start (whether you use the proxy system or not), and disciplining yourself to walk away if the bids go over your limit.

There are very few truly one-of-a-kind items out there. If you're bidding on something and the high bid passes your limit, let it go and search for another listing for that item. I found a pair of earrings once that I just *had* to have. They had a "suggested retail" price of $250, a starting bid of 99 cents, and I was willing to pay $25 or $30 for them. But somebody else wanted them, too. The bidding passed $30 and kept creeping up. I broke my own rule and kept thinking things like, "It's only a dollar more, and they're so cute." When the bid got up to $46, I came to my senses and let the earrings go. Then I did a search, found the exact same earrings from another seller, and got them for $12.50.

Regardless of whether you use a proxy system or bid manually, keep in mind that most people bid in whole, round numbers such as $12 or $25. Entering an odd number, such as $12.39 or $25.07, will increase your chances of outbidding someone by just a few pennies.

Placing Bids at the Last Second

Besides being the name of a species of birds, the traditional meaning of the word "snipe" is to shoot at individuals from a concealed place. In the online auction world, it means to place a high bid in the closing seconds of an auction so that other bidders don't have time to bid again. It's sneaky, but valid—and part of what makes auction buying so much fun.

One way to avoid getting sniped is to place a proxy bid for the full amount you're willing to pay. If the sniper bids less than that amount, your bid will be increased automatically. While this is a safe alternative to manual bidding, it has its drawbacks. Many experienced bidders feel that bidding early calls attention to an item and encourages other buyers to place bids and drive up the price. In fact, many knowledgeable eBayers won't bid until the final few minutes of an auction to keep the final price as low as possible. If you decide to take this approach, use the "watch this item" link to monitor the auction in your My eBay section.

You can also browse your favorite categories using the "ending soonest" sort feature.

Serious snipers often use programs that will place their last-minute bids. Some of the most popular are: eSnipe (www.esnipe.com), Power-Snipe (www.powersnipe.com), AuctionBlitz (www.auctionblitz.com), and AuctionSniper (www.auctionsniper.com). There's a charge for these services, of course, but users swear the savings more than make up for the cost of the sniping service.

You Won—What Happens Next?

When an eBay auction closes, all bidders receive a notice letting them know that the auction is over, what the final sale price was, and whether or not they won. Most other auction sites issue similar notices. Most sellers will also send an immediate notification to the winner with payment instructions and an invoice. To avoid negative feedback or a non-paying bidder complaint, pay promptly. If for any reason you can't pay promptly, communicate with the seller to make appropriate arrangements.

When the item arrives, leave appropriate feedback for the seller. Assuming you are satisfied, offer a specific positive statement, such as "fast shipping," "great communications," or "exactly as described," letting other buyers know what kind of service to expect from that seller. Many sellers will not leave feedback for you until you have left theirs, so don't delay.

You may choose to leave neutral feedback if the product was satisfactory but the seller did not communicate well or ship promptly. Reserve negative feedback for unsatisfactory situations such as gross misrepresentation or the seller not shipping the product, and only leave negative feedback after the situation is resolved as completely as it's going to be.

The seller should also leave feedback for you. Because positive feedback is so important on eBay, don't be shy about asking a seller to post feedback—especially after you have paid for and received the item, and left feedback for the seller.

When Things Go Wrong

Though most eBay and other online auction transactions go smoothly, there may be a time when you don't receive what you were expecting or the item is defective. If this happens, review the seller's return policy to see what recourse you have. The majority of sellers will let you return an item for a refund within a certain amount of days, minus the shipping fees. You may be able to recover the shipping fees if the item was misrepresented in the auction description or damaged during shipping. The very first item I ever sold on eBay was damaged beyond repair by the post office. Because it was insured, I immediately issued the buyer a full refund and filed a claim, and about six weeks later received a check for the amount the item sold for plus the postage. The buyer was disappointed about the damage, but knew that it wasn't my fault and left me very positive feedback. I did the same for her, because she put forth the effort on her end to begin the claim process and turn the damaged package over to the post office.

Before leaving feedback, send the seller a nonconfrontational note explaining why you are dissatisfied, and ask if he will accept a return. Most sellers will try to work with you to bring the transaction to a satisfactory conclusion, and when that happens, you should reward them with positive feedback.

Unfortunately, there are a handful of sellers who really don't care what your problem is—you have it, you own it, deal with it. To them, "all sales are final" means "you are stuck." If the seller is uncooperative and is truly at fault, you are not totally without recourse. If you used a credit card or PayPal, dispute the charge. If you believe fraud was involved, report the seller to eBay. And, of course, you can always leave negative feedback to alert other bidders to the potential for problems with a particular seller.

The Good, the Bad, and the Bargains of Online Auctions

BEFORE YOU START DOING A LOT OF SHOPPING THROUGH online auctions, be sure you've considered all the advantages and drawbacks. This relatively new marketplace is still in many ways a frontier brimming with opportunities and yet with plenty of pitfalls. Understanding the pros and cons will make it easier to get great deals without getting taken.

An Infinite Variety

On the plus side, online auctions are a great source for both new and used items, as well as hard-to-find things. And the auction sites' search engines make it easy for you find out if what you want is up for sale.

Online auctions also give you access to literally millions of sellers on one site. These sellers can be individuals, small businesses, or big corporations. As the buyer, it's your responsibility to know who you're dealing with and what their policies are.

Remember, when you buy on eBay, you are not making your purchase from eBay—you are buying from the seller, who could be an individual just trying to get the garage cleared out or a large multimillion-dollar corporation that uses eBay as one of several sales venues. Does this matter? It depends on what you want and need.

If you're buying a piece of used electronic equipment from an individual, you're not likely to get much in the way of after-the-sale support. But if you know what you're buying, understand the seller's limitations, and are getting a good deal, you can probably live with that. Also, while you aren't technically making the purchase from the auction site, most sites such as eBay will try to help resolve a dispute between users.

While it's possible to have a bad experience on eBay, QuikDrop area developer Tracey Keller points out that the problem is not the online auction site, but rather the people involved. "eBay is a good place," she says. Her advice on all online auction sites, "New buyers should look for the simple transactions and buy from the seller with the best feedback. Read the description carefully, follow the steps in bidding and paying, and your first experiences will be good ones, and you'll keeping on shopping there."

Always check the seller's feedback rating (discussed in the previous chapter) before placing a bid or making a purchase. Virtually all the auction sites and many of the online malls have feedback systems to let you know what kind of reputation the seller has. This is a benefit to online shopping that doesn't exist in the brick-and-mortar world. After all, how often have you walked into a retail store and seen a notice posted on the door that said "X Percent of Our Customers Are Happy with Our Service," followed up with proof and specific comments (both good and bad) from those customers?

There's no way to prove this, but I think it's possible that most online auction sellers have a higher customer satisfaction rating than most retail stores—and it's because that rating is there for the entire world to see. Online auction sellers know that too much negative feedback can put them out of business, so they work hard at providing a level of customer service that will earn them positive feedback ratings.

Now, there are "feedback monsters" out there—buyers who try to bully sellers into doing things that are unreasonable by threatening to leave negative feedback. Some sellers will cave; others won't. My advice to you is to always be fair and reasonable in your evaluation of a seller. If you do find it necessary to leave negative feedback, do it in a calm, professional way, and only after you have exhausted every other means to make the transaction satisfactory. And consider neutral feedback (which doesn't count for or against the rating) if you thought the transaction had some noncritical shortcomings.

I've been fortunate that I've never had to leave negative feedback and only left neutral feedback once. In that case, the seller went on vacation before her auction closed and didn't ship for almost two weeks after I'd won the auction and paid her. The product itself was fine—when I finally received it. I didn't feel that she earned my praise, but I also didn't think she deserved a negative rating. So I left neutral feedback that said, "Merchandise as described; slow shipping." That was a fair warning to others.

I've said this before, but it bears repeating: Your auction bid is a contract, so never bid on something if you are not absolutely certain you are willing to accept the terms of the seller and pay whatever amount you bid. The reality is that you aren't likely to get sued if you back out of an online auction transaction (although it's probably possible—anybody can sue anybody else for just about anything), but doing so repeatedly can get you kicked off the auction site.

Also, be sure you understand the mechanics of the bidding process. A friend of mine told me about a fellow he knew who liked Jaguars (the expensive cars, not the live animal)—and placed winning bids on *eleven* of them on eBay because he didn't realize his bids were actually being entered into the system.

Avoid the Battle of a Bidding War

Perhaps the biggest drawback to online auctions is auction fever, which I discussed in the previous chapter. I cannot stress enough how easy it is to get caught in a bidding war and pay far more than you should for something.

If you do get in a bidding war, take a minute to check out the other bidder (or bidders) to get a sense of her buying patterns and if she appears to be willing to pay top dollar for items. You might be able to get an idea from her purchasing history whether or not you should keep bidding or walk away and wait for the next opportunity.

Know Who Your Friends Are

If you have friends or relatives who might be bidding on the same things you shop for, be sure you know their User IDs. Charlene Davis, my friend and co-author of *Make Big Profits on eBay*, tells a story of finding a vintage wall thermometer on eBay that she knew her father would enjoy. She got into a bidding war with someone who appeared to be as determined as she was to get this item. The price went up—and then she got an e-mail from her father, saying, "Hey, you just outbid me on the thermometer!" She told him to stop bidding, and she won the auction. At first, neither father nor daughter realized they were bidding against each other, but fortunately he finally recognized her User ID.

Don't Wait to Resolve a Problem

When you have a problem with an online auction purchase, take immediate action to resolve it. Certainly you want to give the seller a reasonable opportunity to correct the situation, but if it becomes apparent that he's not going to, begin pursuing your various dispute resolution options. While I was writing this book, I mentioned the topic to a friend, and she said, "Oh, maybe you can help me with a problem I had with an eBay seller." It seems that she bought a necklace that she paid for with a money order (not a good idea) because she was having problems with her PayPal account. (I didn't quite follow that but she said it had been fixed so I didn't worry about it.) The seller never shipped and never responded to my friend's follow-up e-mails. I asked my friend if she had used any of eBay's buyer assistance and protection programs; she said no. Had she left negative feedback? No. Then she dropped the last bit of information: this situation had happened close to a year and a half before. I told her to consider the money paid to the nonperforming seller a donation and forget about it, because so much time had passed.

Don't Blame the Seller for Your Mistakes

While there are some auction sellers who deliberately try to mislead you with their descriptions, there are also many auction buyers who don't pay attention to details and are then disappointed. A friend of mine bought a pair of dance shoes on eBay; when they arrived, she couldn't get her feet into them because they were a size 8N—that's "N" as in narrow. She complained to the seller, who pointed out that the size was clearly stated in the description and refused to accept a return.

Now, if I were advising the seller, I would suggest that she take the shoes back and refund the purchase price but not the shipping. That's just good customer service. But the seller was totally in the right in not doing that because the terms of her auction were clear. Don't expect sellers to do more than they say they will—and don't blame them when they won't.

The bottom line on online auctions is simple: You can get super bargains on just about anything, but you need to be a savvy shopper and pay attention.

Finding What You Want Online

When you walk into a retail store, there are three ways you can find what you want: you can ask someone, you can check out the store directory, or you can just wander around until you see what you're looking for.

Your options with online shopping are similar. You can "ask someone" by doing specific searches, or you can just browse around the internet hoping to find what you want. Doing a specific search is pretty much the same as when you walk into a store, go straight to the product you want to buy, pick it up, pay for it, and leave. Browsing online is much like browsing in a brick-and-mortar store. You can walk around, look at things, go from store to store if necessary, and then make your selection.

So in many ways, visiting an online store is much like visiting a real-world store. The home page and often most of the underlying pages will include not only information on the product you're looking for but also details about other products. It's just like walking into a department store to look for one thing and having to get past all the other displays first. If you're looking for one thing in particular, don't let these extraneous displays distract you. On the other hand, if you're browsing, click on the various links and see what the merchant has to offer.

With that said, it's also important to note that the sheer volume of what's available on the internet can make online searching an overwhelming task. Just as a test, I did a Google search on "dress" and got 68 million results. So I modified my search to "designer dress," and the results dropped to 5.7 million. The problem is that Google doesn't know if I'm looking for dress as a noun (something to wear), a verb (something to do), or an adjective (as in "dress shoes"). When I searched on "Donna Karan designer dress," the results dropped to about 500,000. When I went to Froogle, Google's shopping site, and did the same refined search, I got 46 results.

The lesson here is that you need to understand the various search engines and know how to choose the words you search on to find what you want.

How Search Engines Work

When you hear people talk about doing a search on the internet, they are probably using a search engine.

Search engines have been around for decades, but consumer awareness of what they do and how to use them has only developed in the last decade or so. Every internet search site uses a search engine that it either developed itself or purchased from a third party. There is no standard

What's a Search Engine

Technically, a search engine is a software program that searches a database, gathers information, and then generates reports based on specified terms. The term has become synonymous with the web site on which the search engine operates. For example, Google is a web site (www.google.com) where you can perform internet searches that are executed by Google's search engine software. Essentially, it's a search site powered by a search engine, but it's commonly known as a search engine.

search engine—the various programs find and index material, as well as respond to user queries, in dramatically different ways. Search on Google and on Lycos, for example, using precisely the same keywords, and you'll likely get very different results.

The better-known general search engine sites include: Google (www.google.com), Yahoo! (www.yahoo.com), AltaVista (www.altavista.com), Lycos (www.lycos.com), Ask Jeeves (www.ask.com), and Dogpile (www.dogpile.com). There are also subscription-based search engines, such as LexisNexis (www.lexisnexis.com) which provides legal, news, and business information, and Westlaw (www.westlaw.com), which provides legal information. But the search engines you'll most likely use are free—to you.

Understand, however, that search engine sites are businesses that need revenue to operate, and they make their money by selling advertising. Those ads might come up on searches in boxes clearly marked as advertisements, or they might come up as "sponsored links" that are part of your search results. Typically sponsored links are sold on a pay-per-click basis. That means that if you click on the link, the search engine charges the advertiser. Sponsored links usually are shown on top of or to the side of the real search results. You may or may not want to explore these sites; just be sure you understand that you're responding to an ad and not to the regular search results.

Typically, Google and Yahoo! put the ads along the right side of the search engine results, although sometimes sponsored links will appear above the nonpaid results. In both cases, the sponsored links are noted as such. Other search engines may list the sponsored links above the web results. There's no reason why you shouldn't check out these paid links, although you will find that they often have nothing to do with what you're searching for. Just be sure that you always know who you're dealing with before you provide any personal information or make a purchase.

How to Use Online Search Engines

Though you have choices when it comes to search engines, most people tend to find one that they are comfortable using, and stick with that. Once you understand how search engines work, use several of them and decide which ones you like best.

You may wonder why some sites come up high on the search engines' rankings, and others don't. In part, it's because of how the search engine is programmed. But much of the responsibility for search engine ranking falls to the individual company web sites. If those web sites are not set up in a way that allows the search engines to find them, they're not going to come up in search results.

For example, search engines can't read graphics; they look for text that tells them what a site is about. If they can't find text or find only a little, the site is not going to get a high ranking. Some sites may appear to have a lot of text when you view them, but the search engine spiders (little software robots that search engines use to review and index the content on web sites) can't read it because of the format the text is in. This doesn't mean there's anything wrong with the company or its products—it's just that the web site designer did not create a site that the search engines could find and understand. Smart e-tailers make their sites as appealing as possible to the search engines so that you can find them when you're looking for whatever they sell.

Most of the major search engine sites are very user-friendly. For the most part, all you have to do is type the name of the item you're looking for and click on "search," and you'll be rewarded with a list of thousands of sites.

Results from major search engines often include general information about the product you're looking for as well as sites where the product is sold. For example, you might get listings for industry organization and trade publications that will provide information you can use in making a buying decision. Take the time to browse around those sites even though you probably can't buy on them.

You should also check out the manufacturer's web site, even though it may not sell direct to the consumer. You'll usually find plenty of valuable product information and often links to retailers that carry the product. To find the manufacturer's web site, try typing the company name between www. and .com; most of the time, you'll get what you're looking for. If you don't, use a search engine.

Check out the web sites of the various retailers who carry what you're looking for. It's not uncommon for retailers to have as much or more information on their sites as the manufacturers do. If the retailer has a brick-and-mortar store, don't assume that the online inventory and store inventory will match. In most cases, the online inventory is much larger and more varied. If you're looking for something that you want to go pick up, call first to make sure it's in stock.

Keywords, Modifiers, and Quotes

To find what you want, you need to put the right words into the search engine. Choose your keywords carefully; be descriptive and specific. Searching on "baseball merchandise" will get millions of results. Be more specific—"Major League Baseball merchandise" or even "Major League Baseball clothing"—and you'll get a shorter list of results that are more likely to be what you're interested in.

For an even closer match, try a phrase search. When you enter your keywords into the search box, put quotes around them. For example, when I typed "Major League Baseball clothing" into Google's search box without quotes, I got 1.7 million results because I got every site that had those four words in any order. But when I put quotes around the same words in the search box, the results dropped to 2,500. When you

When You Have a Catalog

When you have a print catalog and know what you want, you can usually search the company's web site by item number and get your order placed quickly. Typically, the site will ask for some codes from the mailing label on the catalog so the merchant can track its marketing efforts. Of course, in addition to ordering by item number, you may still want to browse around the site just to be sure it doesn't have something you want that's not in the catalog.

put quotes around two or more words in a search, you will only get results for that exact phrase.

Every search engine has an advanced search feature. Take the time to figure out how it works, and you'll make your search efforts far more efficient and productive.

Shopping the Shopping Search Engines

You can use the major general search engines when you're shopping, but you'll get more targeted results and probably save time if you use sites designed for shoppers. These sites help you find out information about products, read product evaluations, compare prices, and find sellers.

Shopping search engines can be a bit overwhelming, so get familiar with them and decide which ones you prefer before you do any serious shopping. Think about when you've gone into a large brick-and-mortar shopping mall for the first time—you didn't know exactly what the mall had to offer, you weren't sure where certain stores were, and when you went into a store, you had to figure out how the merchandise was arranged. Some of the better-known shopping sites include Froogle (www.froogle.com), Shopzilla (www.shopzilla.com), BizRate (www.bizrate.com), PriceGrabber (www.pricegrabber.com), Shopping.com (www.shopping.com), and Consumer World.org (www.consumerworld.org).

If you'd prefer to buy from a local merchant—whether online or in person—you can still shop online. Check out www.shoplocal.com; just type in your zip code or city and state, and you can search for products anywhere in a 1- to 50-mile radius. You can search by category, brand, price range, or retailer; then choose whether you want to buy online on in-store.

Chapter 7

What You Can't—or Shouldn't—Buy Online

THERE IS VERY LITTLE THAT YOU CAN'T BUY—OR AT LEAST shop for—online. But there are a few things that are not available online—and other things that might be available but shouldn't be. If you use good judgment and don't do anything in the online world that you know would be objectionable in the real world, you shouldn't have any problems.

Online Auction Sites Have the Most Rules

When you are buying directly from a seller on that individual's or company's web site, it's up to you to determine if your transaction is acceptable and legal. When you're buying on an online auction or an online mall, you have an extra degree of protection because the sellers are restricted by the site's rules. That doesn't mean every seller follows the rules—in fact, there are always some that don't. Some of the violations are accidental, some are intentional. If you see an online auction seller breaking the rules, take a few minutes to file a report with the auction site so the situation can be corrected.

Every auction site has a list of prohibited items, and if you have any questions about what you're buying, check that list. In general, when shopping online auctions, don't try to buy

- anything that might be counterfeit (such as fake designer items) or stolen.
- anything that might violate a copyright or trademark, or violate the rights or privacy of another person.
- anything that might cause harm to another person, in particular, a minor.
- illegal drugs and drug paraphernalia.
- human bodies, body parts, and bodily fluids.
- animals, including pets and livestock.
- any item that has been recalled by a government agency or its manufacturer and, therefore, may be unsafe.
- any item that would most likely be used to commit some sort of crime.

If It's Illegal, Don't Buy It

A good rule to follow when it comes to what you shouldn't try to buy online is this: If it's illegal for you to purchase or possess the item, don't try to buy it online.

- any item that would be prohibited by government regulations.

Most auction sites also prohibit a number of items that might not necessarily be illegal but the site has decided for the safety of its users to forbid those items. Examples of such items include weapons and accessories, fireworks, prescription drugs, and law enforcement items.

Buying Weapons Online

Firearms and other weapons are readily available online. The way online firearm purchases are typically handled is that you find the gun you want online and make the purchase according to the terms of the seller. The gun is then shipped to a licensed dealer in your area. You can pick up the gun from that dealer after completing all the necessary paperwork. Sales of other weapons by legitimate dealers are handled in a similar manner in accordance with appropriate regulations.

Online Sales of Tobacco Products and Alcoholic Beverages

Tobacco products—defined as cigars, cigarettes, smokeless tobacco, pipe tobacco, and roll-your-own tobacco—are readily available on the internet. The Alcohol and Tobacco Tax and Trade Bureau of the U.S. Department of the Treasury has no special rules for the online sale of these items; however, they are subject to the laws of the states where the seller and buyer are located.

You can also find web sites selling a wide range of wine, beer, and spirits, but whether or not you can buy them online depends on where

If It's from Spam, Don't Buy It

Never, ever buy anything from unsolicited spam e-mail. Never.

you're located. The seller must be in compliance with all applicable federal regulations as well as the laws of the states where the seller and the buyer are located. Sellers of alcoholic beverages will usually post all the appropriate information and restrictions on their web sites, so you can tell before you even try to place an order if they'll ship to you.

Buying from Foreign Countries

THE INTERNET MAKES GLOBAL SHOPPING EASY, BUT WHAT do you need to know about buying from sellers in foreign countries? For a substantial percentage of consumer items purchased from large corporations, you aren't likely to see much difference if you buy from a company overseas than if you buy from one in the United States. And most of those companies will have a U.S. presence anyway, even though the product may actually ship from another country.

When you make a purchase from a company based overseas, you need to keep in mind that it is not governed by U.S. consumer protection laws. Many foreign-based companies are legitimate and want to reach the U.S. market, so they will provide a high level of customer service and voluntarily abide by our rules. But there are always those operators that will provide substandard products and services because they know they can get away with it, and they're not interested in long-term customers who provide repeat business.

Begin—as always—with knowing who you are dealing with. Identify the company's name, its physical address, a telephone number, and an e-mail address. Check to see if the company is affiliated with industry groups, trust and safety programs, or other self-regulatory programs you are familiar with. Next, be sure about what you're buying. Look for accurate, clear, and easily accessible information about the goods or services being offered. If you have questions, contact the company for clarification before you make a purchase. Think about this: if you can't understand the answers you get, it might be a good idea to buy elsewhere. Christopher Faulkner, president and founder of CI Host, says it is a lot harder to get a refund from an overseas seller than a U.S.-based one, so do your best in advance to eliminate the need for a possible refund.

International Payments and Foreign Currencies

The seller should clearly designate the currency involved so you'll know whether your need to pay in U.S. dollars or another currency. If it's a foreign currency, be sure to figure out the exchange rate before you buy so you know how much you're really paying.

All major credit cards can process payments to foreign countries. You can make the payment through your bank, but you will probably be charged for the service. Again, do your homework to find out ahead of time what fees and other issues are involved.

How Will the Seller Ship?

Be sure you know how the seller is going to ship and when you can expect delivery. Many of the major U.S. carriers—DHL, FedEx, UPS, etc.—operate internationally. The seller may also use the local postal system in the country of origin that will then connect with the U.S. Postal Service. Find out about insurance and what will happen if the package is lost or damaged.

Customs, Duty, and Taxes

Depending on what you buy and its value, you may have to pay duty (or tax) to the U.S. government when you import it. A legitimate seller will tell you what to expect. If you're not sure, contact the U.S. Customs office at www.customs.gov or call (877) 287-8667 for more information. You may also need import licenses or other permits to bring the merchandise into the United States. Again, the U.S. Customs office or a customs broker can help you.

Consumer Protection Issues

WHEN I TALK WITH PEOPLE WHO DON'T SHOP ONLINE AND ask why not, the two most common answers I hear are: One, they're not comfortable using their credit cards online; and two, they are just generally afraid of getting ripped off. Both of these are generally groundless fears.

The best advice for online shopping—actually, for shopping in any venue—is to trust your instincts. If something doesn't seem right, if the deal is too good to be true, if you can't verify the information about the

Stay Safe Online

A great web site with information about staying safe online for people of all ages is www.getnetwise.org. The site is a project of some internet industry companies and public interest organizations, and it has a lot of good basic information. Another good site is www.onguardonline.gov, a joint project of the federal government and the technology industry. The site includes tips, articles, videos, and quizzes, as well as where to report spam or a scam and how to sign up for periodic computer security alerts. You should also take a look at the Federal Citizen Information Center's Consumer Action web site at www.consumeraction.gov. The site includes consumer tips, fraud trends, and more.

seller, then don't make the purchase. You can always buy somewhere else. When you find yourself tempted to make a purchase because you want to take advantage of a great deal before it disappears, remember that there will always be more great deals. And it's better that you miss out on a great deal once in a while than make a bad decision that costs you a substantial amount of money.

Set Up an E-Mail Address Exclusively for Online Shopping

When you begin shopping online, your volume of junk e-mail and spam is going to increase. Even though you check merchant privacy policies, even though you tell sites you don't want to receive e-mail, the reality is that your name, address, and the fact that you buy on the internet is going to get captured and sold.

The solution is to create an e-mail address that you use exclusively for online shopping. When the level of junk mail gets too high for you to deal with, close that account and open another one. There are countless sites that offer free e-mail addresses, and they're quick and easy to set up. Internet service providers like America Online allow users to set up multiple e-mail addresses, so if you're using a paid service, see if you can add an online shopping address. Save your permanent e-mail address for friends and business associates, not online shopping.

Paying with a Credit Card Is the Safest Way to Shop

You are at less risk for unauthorized use of your credit card when you are shopping online than when you give your card to a server in a restaurant or shopping in a mall. CI Host's Christopher Faulkner says that "old-fashioned dumpster diving" is how many criminals get credit card numbers—they pick through the trash looking for receipts that contain a complete card number. Or a restaurant server or store clerk may copy the number and then use your card before you realize it's been compromised. These situations are just not an issue when you're shopping online.

"It's happened to me, and I'm a cyber security expert," says Faulkner. He was in Las Vegas when his credit card number was copied by a server in a hotel restaurant. "She had friends that worked at different places around Las Vegas, some clothing stores and other places. They racked up about $10,000 on my credit card over the course of two days by going in and keying in the number by hand on the store's terminal."

The chances of something similar happening with an online purchase are slim. "I've never had my credit card misused through an online merchant," Faulkner says. "I spend, with my company's credit card and my own credit card, several million dollars a year through online purchases. The only instance I have ever had of my credit card number being compromised came through a direct, face-to-face interaction with another human being."

As I suggested in Chapter 2, consider getting one credit card that you use exclusively for online purchases. Faulkner agrees with that advice. "I have one credit card that I use for all of my online purchases," he says. "Then I watch that account very closely to ensure that I have not been scammed or duped in any way. If you have multiple credit cards, pick one and use that for online shopping only. That way you can log onto the web site with that credit card company's online banking system and you can check out your account routinely [rather than once a month when your statement arrives], and you don't have to check several different credit cards for different charges. If you are using the same credit card for all of your online purchases and you do see a fake charge, all you do is charge it back and close that credit card account. It's not a big deal."

A number of credit card issuers offer one-time use credit card numbers (called "virtual account numbers," "secure online account numbers," or "controlled payment numbers") that let you shop online without using your real credit card number. When you use this service, your credit card company generates a substitute number to take the place of your real account number, so your real account number is never given to the online merchant. Charges will appear on your credit card statement just like any other transaction. If the site you're shopping with experiences a security breach, the substitute number would be worthless and your real number would not be compromised.

Make Your Payment Securely

When it's time to pay, most online merchants will direct you to an area of their site that's secure. A safe site will show a symbol of an unbroken key, a picture of a closed lock, or a web address that begins with "https." (That letter "s" is important.) In addition to these symbols, most browsers will display a warning message that will let you know whether you're sending to a secure or unsecure site before you send any information. These secure pages encrypt the information that is being exchanged. The process slows down the server, which is why it isn't practical for every page on a site to be secure. Pages that are just displaying images and text about products don't need this level of security. If you have any question about the safety measures of a site or if the site does not indicate that it's secure, don't place your order or send your information.

> ## What Online Sellers Must Do
>
> Online sellers are subject to the same federal, state, and local regulations that apply to any company. Of course, you need to be sure you're dealing with a legitimate company and that you know where it's located to be protected by these regulations.
>
> In general, online merchants must accurately and honestly represent their products and services (to avoid charges of fraud) and ship within 30 days (or tell you that it will take longer). Most online transactions go smoothly, but you should know what to do if yours doesn't.

Never send your credit card information in an e-mail. E-mails are not secure transmissions; you may as well write your card number and expiration date on a post card and drop it in the mail.

Many e-tailers will give you the option of establishing an account that will remember your name, address, and other information when you return to the site. This can be a tremendous convenience when ordering, especially if it's a site you expect to buy from regularly. But while there's relatively little risk in storing your name and delivery address, don't let the site store your credit card information. When you pay with a credit card, the merchant keeps the number only long enough to process the transaction unless you approve of the number being entered into a database. That, says Faulkner, can be risky. If the merchant's web site is hacked, your financial information could be stolen.

When Things Go Wrong

When you make an online purchase and there's a problem, your first step should be to contact the seller. In most cases, you'll be guided to a quick and easy resolution. For example, I once ordered a set of six napkin rings that were made of wood carved into different wild animal shapes.

The nose of the giraffe was broken off when I took the napkin rings out of the package. Though I found the nose in the bottom of the box, I didn't want to glue it back on. I sent the company an e-mail, explained the problem, told them I'd like to have the item replaced, and asked how they wanted to proceed. I was willing to return the broken item or the entire set (at their expense, of course) for a replacement. Within hours, I received an e-mail reply with an apology and telling me that they would ship a complete new set at no charge, and it wasn't necessary to return the broken item. Have I bought from that company again? You bet. They're a class act and they've earned my business.

Another organization I buy from often is the Susan G. Komen Breast Cancer Foundation (www.komen.org). They have a nice selection of pink ribbon products that I buy for myself and as gifts, and a percentage of the purchase price goes to breast cancer research. A watch I bought from the site stopped working just a few weeks after I got it. I had a jeweler check the battery and that wasn't the problem. I sent an e-mail to the address indicated in my order confirmation (which I saved), explained the situation, and asked what the procedure was. I got a prompt response saying that a replacement watch was being shipped and they would be sending me a postage-paid label so I could return the defective watch. Another class act—one that also does a lot of good. I highly recommend it.

On another occasion, I bought a reconditioned Hewlett Packard fax/copier/scanner/printer combo unit on eBay. The same unit was selling new in office supply stores for about $400; the reconditioned unit on eBay was $185 plus $30 shipping and came with a one-year factory warranty. When the machine arrived, we couldn't get it to work. I e-mailed the eBay seller; he promptly responded with Hewlett Packard's toll-free service number. My husband got on the phone with the HP technician, who walked him through several unsuccessful exercises to try to get the machine to work. Finally, he gave up, apologized profusely, and said he would send us a new machine. He said that in the box with the machine would be a return label; all we had to do was put the defective unit in the box, seal it up, put the label on, and either call UPS for a pickup or take it to any UPS drop point. The replacement arrived a couple of days later, we swapped out the machines, and more than two years later that unit is still working fine. It was a minor inconvenience, but it was something that could not have been predicted and was handled with tremendous courtesy and efficiency.

The point of these three stories is to say this: Give your sellers a reasonable chance to fix the problem before you get upset and angry. Have I had problems with e-tailers that were not so easily resolved? Yes. You probably will, too. But start by assuming the merchant is going to do the right thing.

Let's look at some of the more common problems that are likely to occur with online purchases.

Orders Not Shipped on Time or at All

Savvy online sellers are avoiding this problem by setting up automated systems that let you know when your package has been shipped and how you can track it. You may be eager to get your merchandise, but once it's shipped, it's out of the seller's hands, so be patient. If the merchant doesn't provide you with shipping information within a few days of receiving your order, contact the customer service department (usually an e-mail will be sufficient) and ask for a status report. In most cases, you'll be told one of four things: the merchandise is backordered, sold out, discontinued, or on its way. For the first three situations, the merchant should give you the option of waiting until the item is available or canceling your order. If it's been shipped, you should be given a carrier name and tracking number.

Lost Shipments

It doesn't happen often, but occasionally carriers will lose shipments. In most cases, the merchant will work with you and the carrier to either find the package or replace the order. You might run into the occasional seller who says essentially, "It was shipped, we have proof, we've done what we're required to do, and you're on your own." You can still try to trace the package with the carrier, but if you are unsuccessful, your quickest and easiest recourse is to dispute the charge on your credit card—and don't buy from that company again. The better online retailers will, after a reasonable time, replace your order and take care of filing a claim with the carrier on their end.

Unwanted or Defective Merchandise

Years ago, a popular scam was for mail order merchants to send unordered products then bill for them and get very aggressive with their collection efforts. Consumers often paid because they didn't know what else to do. Stronger consumer protection laws have virtually eliminated this sleazy tactic. If you receive something you didn't order, it's yours and you don't have to pay for it. With that said, if the merchant made an honest mistake and shipped something in error, you have a moral obligation to either return the product or pay for it.

The category of unwanted merchandise can also include items that don't fit, don't look or function like you thought they would, aren't of the quality you expected, are defective, or fail to satisfy you for a number of other reasons. Contact the merchant's customer service department, explain the situation, and ask for instructions on how to return the item. Most of the time, the process will go smoothly. If the problem is the merchant's fault—the wrong item was shipped or the product is defective—it's reasonable to expect the merchant to pay any return shipping fees. They may do that by sending you a prepaid shipping label or arranging for the pickup of the package from their end, or you may have to pay for the shipping and request a refund. If there's nothing wrong with the merchandise but you just don't like it, you'll probably end up paying the return shipping charges—although some companies will provide free return shipping.

In most cases, returning an item ordered online is a simple, routine matter. In fact, most online retailers include complete return instructions with every shipment.

Unresponsive Retailers

It doesn't happen often, but there could be times when you have a problem, you call and send e-mails, and the merchant ignores you or refuses to solve the problem to your satisfaction. If you paid by credit card, dispute the charge. Call the customer service number on your credit card statement (or check to see if you can make the dispute online), provide a brief synopsis of the problem, and ask for a credit. The credit card company will remove the charge from your account and contact the merchant. In many cases, the merchants will respond to this type of pressure by doing what they should have done in the first place—whether it's a replacement, refund, or whatever. In most cases, the only way the credit card company will reinstate the charge is if the merchant can prove that it met its responsibilities and obligations to you.

If you didn't pay by credit card or if your credit card company won't help, you can try using an online dispute resolution service such as SquareTrade (www.squaretrade.com). If that doesn't work, and the dollar amount is high enough to make it worth it, file a traditional lawsuit.

Dealing with Credit Card Billing Errors

If your credit card is billed for merchandise you returned or never received, if you were charged twice for the same item, or if you were charged the wrong amount, you can take advantage of the dispute settlement procedures provided by the federal Fair Credit Billing Act (FCBA). These procedures only apply to billing errors, not to disputes about the quality of goods and services (although most credit card companies will help you in that case).

The FCBA covers these types of billing disputes: unauthorized charges (federal law limits your responsibility to $50; most credit card companies don't charge that even though they can); charges that list the wrong date or amount; charges for goods and services you didn't accept or that weren't delivered as agreed; math errors; failure to post payments and other credits such as returns; and charges for which you ask for an explanation or written proof of purchase along with a claimed error or request for clarification.

If you see a billing error on your credit card statement, write to the creditor (card issuer) at the address given for billing inquiries, not the address for sending payments. You may call the creditor, but you have to send a letter to be protected under the law. Include your name, address, account number, and a description of the billing error. Your letter must reach the creditor within 60 days after the first bill containing the error was mailed to you—which is why you should always check your credit card statements carefully when they arrive. It's a good idea to send your letter by certified mail, return receipt requested. Include copies (not originals) of receipts and any other documents that support your claim. Keep a copy of the letter for your files.

Unless the problem has already been resolved, the creditor must acknowledge your complaint in writing within 30 days of receiving it and resolve the dispute within two billing cycles but not more than 90 days after receiving your letter.

While your claim is being investigated, you may withhold payment on the disputed amount and the creditor may not take any legal or other action to collect that amount. If the investigation shows that there was indeed an error, the creditor must explain in writing what steps will be taken, including crediting your account for the mistake as well as all finance charges, late fees, or other charges related to the error. If the creditor determines the bill is correct, you must be told promptly and in writing what you owe and why. If you disagree, you have ten days to notify the creditor and request further investigation. Creditors that fail to follow these procedures are subject to penalties.

Online Buyer Protection Programs

More and more auction and shopping sites, as well as online payment services, are offering buyer protection programs. Before you count on one of these programs, read the terms and be sure you understand exactly what it will and won't do.

Be a Responsible Online Shopper

I've told you what the seller is obligated to do, but there are two parties to every online transaction. Do your part to make sure that your purchase goes smoothly—and be prepared to take action if it doesn't.

Keep Good Records

The most important thing you should do after you've made your purchase is to maintain good records. Keep receipts and order confirmations so you can provide complete information if you need to follow up. One simple way to do this is to print out your order confirmations and keep them in a pending folder, along with printouts of any e-mails you receive with shipping information or other details. When the merchandise arrives, make a note of the delivery date and condition, and move the document to a completed folder. Periodically check the pending folder and follow up on ordered but not received items as necessary. Use the information in the completed folder if you have an issue after delivery, such as a defective product.

Read the Warranty

Always check out the warranty before you buy so you know exactly what is covered if you have a problem later on. Generally, if the product isn't working when you receive it, you can go back to the merchant for a replacement. But if you keep it for a while and then it breaks, you'll probably have to go back to the manufacturer—and the manufacturer will probably want to see some sort of proof of purchase (refer to your completed order folder for all the details). In addition, you may have to ship the product to a repair center.

Don't Answer Questions the Merchant Doesn't Need to Know

Don't provide any more information than you absolutely have to in order to complete the purchase. Yes, you need to give your name, contact details, address, and payment information. You don't need to tell a store your spouse's name, number of kids and pets you have, or what your hobbies are. Many sites will ask for unnecessary data that will be used later for marketing purposes or sold to marketing companies. When filling in an order form, don't automatically answer every question; think about whether it's necessary for you to reveal certain information. The required fields will be indicated as such; if the field isn't required, don't fill it in.

Never give your Social Security number to an online merchant. There is absolutely no reason why it would be needed, and being asked for it is unnecessary. The exception is when you're dealing with online banks and brokerages, but for general online shopping, never reveal your Social Security number.

You Don't Need Fries with That

Resist unnecessary upselling. Many sites will offer you additional products and other add-ons such as service agreements when you begin the checkout process—much like a fast food restaurant clerk tries to sell you fries, chips, a larger drink, or dessert. On some web sites, these items will be checked by default, so you need to "uncheck" them if you don't want to buy. There may be times when the upselling has value—if, for example, you really want the additional products or services. One site I used to buy from regularly totals up each order and tells the buyer how much more she can buy without increasing the shipping charge. The site provides a list of all products within that price range. I think that's a great marketing technique, but only because I see it as adding value without being pushy. I don't happen to shop on that site anymore because of a delivery problem that was compounded by poor customer service—but I still think getting a message that says "You can purchase $14.50 more in merchandise without increasing your shipping charge" with links to everything in the catalog that is $14.50 or less is a great idea.

Protect Your Account Information

As I've mentioned, many online retailers offer the option of setting up an account that will remember you when you come back. Typically, these accounts require a password, and it's important that you safeguard that password. Choose one that isn't easy to guess and includes both letters and numbers. Avoid using a telephone number, birth date, or a portion of your Social Security number as your password. Don't use the same password on multiple sites, and change your passwords on a regular basis. Finally, keep your passwords private. Don't give them to people who don't need to know them.

Watch the Pop-Ups

Never enter personal information on a pop-up screen. A pop-up screen is a window that is displayed on top of the existing page you're viewing—it "pops up" over the current page and displays new information. Most pop-up screens are advertisements that may be generated by the web site you're visiting or if you have adware running on your computer. However, it's possible for pop-up screens to be created by identity thieves and be totally unrelated to the web site you're on. When it's time for you to order and pay, legitimate companies will direct you to a secure page on their site; they don't ask you to enter personal or financial information on a pop-up screen.

What's Real and What's Not

While you should expect to receive an e-mail order confirmation message from an online seller, merchants will not ask *you* to confirm a recent transaction. If you get an e-mail asking you to confirm a purchase, delete it—it's likely a phishing scam (explained in detail in the next chapter) that coincidentally arrived after you were shopping, and it's from a thief who is just trying to get your credit card or banking information.

Don't Get Spied On

One of the biggest threats to your computer and privacy are programs that manage to sneak onto your system and then affect how your computer operates, change the settings, send ads you don't want, and let others see what you're doing online. An increasingly popular tool with identity thieves, these programs are called spyware, adware, malware, hijackware, parasiteware, scumware, and probably a few more similar names. Typically, they're attached to free software that you download. You may not even realize they're on your computer. You can also get these programs through basic activities such as surfing the internet, reading e-mail, instant messages, and downloading music and other files. It's common to unknowingly download adware when you accept an end user license agreement from a software program.

These programs gather your information, such as what web sites you visit and even personal information such as credit card numbers and passwords, and then use your internet connection to relay that data to another computer, where it can be used for a range of reasons from advertising to identity theft. Keylogger programs are less concerned about what sites you visit. They record account numbers, passwords, and other typed-in text. Scumware changes how you view web sites you visit. The software replaces the real content of sites with ads from scumware advertisers with the goal of generating traffic for those advertisers.

Thwart Keylogger Programs

If your computer gets infected with a keylogger program (which is a spyware program that monitors what you type to steal your account numbers, passwords, and other private information), you can still protect yourself. Never type in confidential information. Instead, store your account numbers and passwords in a password-protected document that you keep on a disk or memory card—not on your computer's hard drive. When you need the information, simply access the file, copy the data, and paste it where you need it. All the keystroke logger will be able to determine is that you are copying and pasting, but it won't be able to get the actual information.

The rate of introduction of new types of malicious software is rapidly increasing. The trend is moving away from self-propagating viruses such as worms and shifting to spyware and Trojan horse-type programs that will track your online behavior or allow remote control of your computer. Increasingly, organized crime groups are using this type of software for their own financial gain.

To protect yourself, install at least two spyware-removal programs—it's entirely possible that one will catch something the other will miss. You can find excellent free and for-pay spyware-removal programs at www.download.com. For reviews of the programs, check out www.spywareremoversreview.com.

Keep your spyware-removal program (as well as your anti-virus program) up-to-date. Be cautious when downloading free software—even programs that are sent to you by people you know and trust, because your friends may not realize what they're sending. Don't go browsing around questionable sites, such as those with "adult" material or that offer free downloads of music, software, or other files that you would normally expect to pay for. If a site asks you for permission to download a program that will allow you to view the site better, simply decline—there's an excellent chance that program will include spyware.

Remember that even with two or more good spyware-removal programs running, it's possible for one of these sinister programs to sneak onto your computer. If your system seems to slow down or just isn't performing as usual, or if you see a spike in pop-up messages, immediately update your spyware-removal programs and your anti-virus software and do a full system scan. It's far easier to avoid spyware than it is to find and remove it, so practice "safe computing" whenever you're online.

Don't confuse spyware with cookies. In this context, cookies are not yummy snacks, they are small data files that are sent to your computer when you log onto a web site. They stay on your computer either temporarily for that session only or permanently on your hard drive. They provide a way for the web site to identify you and keep track of your preferences, which can be a good thing. For example, let's say you filled out a form on a web site and decided to leave that page to view another page. With cookies, when you come back to the form page, the data will still be there. Without cookies, the data will be gone and the site won't know who you are.

If you have a cookie from a particular site on your hard drive, when you log onto that site later, the cookie sends your information to the site so it knows who you are. If your user ID and password for that site are stored in a cookie, you won't have to type them again. If your name, address, and billing information are stored in a cookie, it can make ordering much faster and easier. Also, by tracking your shopping habits, cookies allow sites to tailor their pages to your preferences and create a custom online experience for you. Think of cookies like a claim check at a dry cleaner or shoe repair shop. The shop gifts you a claim check (cookie) so that when you come back to pick up your things, it knows who you are and what to give you.

While cookies can be beneficial, they also have a downside. They can contain a considerable amount of personal data, which can make them the object of attack. This is known as cookie poisoning; it happens when a hacker modifies or steals the contents of your cookies to obtain your personal information. Guard against this by keeping your antivirus software up-to-date and being careful about downloading files when you aren't positive what they are.

While it's possible to prevent all cookies from being stored on your computer, to do so severely limits your web surfing experience. The default settings of your web browser typically allow what's known as first-party cookies that do not contain any personal information and are created by the web site you are currently visiting, but do not allow third-party cookies. Third-party cookies are created by a web site other than the one you are visiting, such as an advertiser on that site. These cookies have no direct benefit to you: Their purpose is usually to track your surfing habits, and that's why they're considered an invasion of privacy and a security risk. You can adjust the settings for how your computer accepts and stores cookies in the Options or Preferences menu of your browser.

Learn more about cookies at www.cookiecentral.com. For software that lets you review and control the cookies on your system, visit www.no morecookies.com.

Secure All Your Electronic Devices

I've talked about protecting your computer, but it's important to remember that other electronics may be vulnerable. Many electronic devices, from cell phones to PDAs (personal digital assistants) to video games and even car navigation systems are computers and are subject to the same risks as your desktop or laptop computer. It's possible, for example, for your cell phone to be infected by a virus, for a thief to steal your phone or your wireless service, or for a hacker to access the records on your PDA. Any electronic device that uses some kind of computer-ized component is susceptible to software imperfections and vulnera-bilities, and if the device is connected to the internet (either wired or wireless) or a network, the risk increases.

Although the following suggestions aren't directly related to the process of online shopping, these tips to protect yourself and your equipment are worth sharing:

- *Be aware of physical security.* Don't leave your device unattended in public or in other easily accessible areas. Be alert when you are in crowded situations where it would be easy for someone to steal from you. It's much easier for a thief to gain or corrupt informa-tion when he has physical access to the device.
- *Keep software current.* If the vendor releases any updates or patches for your operating system, install them as soon as possible. This prevents attackers from being able to exploit known bugs and security failures.
- *Protect your data with good passwords.* Choose devices that allow you to password-protect your files, and create passwords that will be difficult for a hacker to guess. Do not choose options that will allow your computer or other device to remember your pass-words.

- *Disable remote connectivity when not in use.* If your device is equipped with wireless technology that allows it to connect to other devices or computers, be sure that feature is turned off when you're not actively using it.
- *Encrypt your files.* If you have encryption software on your device, use it to protect sensitive personal or business information. When files are encrypted, unauthorized people can't view the data even if they gain access to the file. An important note when you use encryption: Be sure to use passwords and passphrases that you can remember; if you forget or lose them, you won't be able to access your data.

Frauds and Scams

I TRULY BELIEVE THAT MOST PEOPLE ARE DECENT AND honest, and because companies are run by people, most of them are decent and honest. But there are always the few who want something for nothing or who think it's okay to steal. The structure of the internet makes it easy for these criminals to hit, run, and hide, so you need to know how to protect yourself from frauds and scams when you're online. Internet fraud losses are in the tens of millions of dollars annually, and the most effective way to avoid becoming a victim is to educate yourself.

The Scoop on Scams

A great resource for information on the latest online scams—and even some offline ones, as well—is Scambusters at www.scam busters.org. Visit the site and sign up for a free e-newsletter that's packed with great information and valuable alerts.

It's fairly easy to detect most online scams: If the offer sounds too good to be true, it probably is. You've probably heard that all your life, and the internet hasn't changed that reality. In fact, a great web site, www.lookstoogoodtobetrue.com, was created by a joint federal law enforcement and industry task force to educate consumers about internet fraud so they won't become victims. Take a look at this web site for the latest information on online frauds and scams and some victim stories—then make a commitment that you won't become a victim yourself.

Identity Theft

Identity theft is one of the fastest growing crimes, and ID theft scammers are happily operating on the internet. But your risk of being a victim of ID theft simply by making purchases on reputable web sites is practically nil. If the site is secure, your personal information should be safe.

The most frequent sources of identity theft are stolen wallets and checkbooks—not credit card numbers pilfered over the internet. However, the problem of identity theft from online "phishing" scams (discussed later in this chapter) is growing.

The problem with identity theft is that the bad guy doesn't just steal one credit card and go on a shopping spree. He (or she) gets new credit cards, takes out new loans, rents items that are not returned, and in general leaves a trail of unpaid bills the victim usually doesn't find out about until a serious amount of damage has been done. It's not uncommon for the identity thief to be someone you know. A Massachusetts woman stole the identity of a friend, obtained several credit cards, and ran up almost $50,000 in debt. She apparently felt guilty about what she'd done, because then she decided to file a fraudulent bankruptcy so her friend wouldn't have to pay the bills. She got caught filing the bankruptcy and went to prison—and her friend (but with friends like this, who needs enemies?) probably spent years cleaning up her credit history.

Identity theft is more likely to be committed offline than online, and often by someone close to the victim. However, accessing your accounts online rather than waiting for mailed monthly paper statements can provide earlier detection of a crime and reduce your losses.

How can you avoid becoming a victim of identity theft? Don't carry your checkbook or Social Security card with you. Don't give out your Social Security number unless there is a valid reason. Don't use your mother's real maiden name or your real city of birth as identifiers. Add security passwords to online and offline accounts so that anyone who tries to impersonate you needs to know more than your name, address, and Social Security number. Have your mail delivered to a locked box and destroy all unsolicited pre-approved credit offers and blank bankcard checks with a crosscut shredder.

Periodically check your credit report for suspicious activity. You can get a free copy of your report from each of the three major credit bureaus once a year. Go to www.annualcreditreport.com to order yours. (Note: do not confuse the site set up to obtain your credit report once a year for free with www.freecreditreport.com, which is a commercial site of Experian, a credit bureau that wants to sell you a credit monitoring service.) Set up a plan to order the reports on a rotating basis every four months so you'll be able to quickly see if any unauthorized accounts have been opened. For example, get your Experian report in January, your Equifax report in May, and your TransUnion report in September. It's easy to do online or by mail.

If you are a victim of identity theft, you need to take swift action. Call the three major credit bureaus, advise them that you are an identity theft victim, and put a fraud alert on your credit file. The bureaus do exchange this sort of information and tell you that when you contact one, the information is relayed to the other two. However, from my own experience of having my identity stolen, it's better to notify all three bureaus separately. (My information was not obtained online; it was taken from the office of the broker who used to handle my retirement account.) When credit bureaus are advised that your identity has been stolen, they will send you a copy of your credit report. Review it carefully and immediately dispute any entries that you don't recognize. Contact those creditors and have the accounts closed immediately. Also, ask for copies of all fraudulent credit applications and billing statements.

Close your affected credit card accounts; the card companies should be able to issue you new cards in a few days. Change the passwords on all your financial accounts.

File a police report, and get a copy of the report. Some local police agencies will be reluctant to accept such a report if you don't know where the identity thief is located. If you meet resistance, ask to file a "for information only" report that doesn't require them to do any investigation. You may need to provide a copy of this report to creditors and/or credit bureaus. Also, the fact that you filed a police report could be helpful when it comes to prosecuting if the perpetrators are found.

When you initially notify the credit bureaus of the problem and ask for a fraud alert to be placed on your account, the alert will stay for 90 days. If you want to extend it, you must re-contact the credit bureaus and make that request. Generally, they will ask for evidence of the crime (the police report you filed is sufficient) before they will extend the fraud alert for a period of years. With the fraud alert on your account, creditors are asked (but not required) to contact you before granting credit or opening a new account. The credit bureaus don't make it easy for you to protect yourself in this way because it also restricts their ability to make money by using your information, so be prepared to invest some time and endure some frustration during this process.

For more information on protecting yourself and your family from identity theft (children and the elderly are often victims), check out the Identity Theft Resource Center at www.idtheftcenter.org.

Sex Products, Fake Designer Watches, Pharmaceuticals, Million-Dollar Business Opportunities, and More

If you have an e-mail address, you're going to get spam. Period. There are ways to reduce the amount of spam (unsolicited commercial e-mail) you get, but it's impossible to avoid it completely.

Here's the rule for online shoppers when it comes to spam: Never, never, never buy anything from an unsolicited e-mail. Never. No matter how good the deal looks, no matter how much you might want whatever it is or whatever it promises, no matter what.

Common Frauds and Scams

The ironic thing about frauds and scams is that for the crime to happen it usually takes some degree of cooperation from the victim. Often it's an unwitting cooperation and the victim doesn't realize it, but it's cooperation nonetheless. So it's a good idea to take a look at some of the common frauds and scams you're likely to encounter online and how to avoid them.

Spoofing and Phishing

The hottest and most troubling scams on the internet are "spoofing" and "phishing" (pronounced "fishing," as in fishing for information). These are bogus e-mails and web sites that try to trick people into revealing personal data that can later be used for fraudulent purposes.

Spoofing or phishing frauds attempt to make people believe that they are receiving e-mail from a specific, trusted source or that they are securely connected to a known, trusted web site when that is not the case. Spoofing also often involves trademark and other intellectual property violations.

In e-mail spoofing, the header of the e-mail appears to have originated from someone or somewhere other than the actual source. Spam distributors and criminals often use spoofing in an attempt to get recipients to open and possibly even respond to their solicitations. There are many, many viruses out there that use spoofing technology. They invade someone's system, grab the address book, then send out e-mails with a malicious file attached to everyone in the address book. You think you're getting something from someone you know, but if you download and open the file, your system will be infected with the virus. It's very easy to forge the "from" address in an e-mail to make it look like the message is from someone you know or a company you do business with.

My personal rule on opening attached files is this: I have to know the sender and the e-mail has to explain what the attached file is and why it's being sent. If something doesn't look right or seems out of character, I create a new e-mail and send it to the person to find out if he really did send me the file. The standard message I put in that e-mail is: "Thank you for the email you sent me indicated above. It contains an attachment that you did not explain the purpose of. In view of the possibility that a virus could have sent this to me without your knowledge, I would appreciate an explanation of the attachment's purpose. As a precaution, I have deleted the attachment, so please send it again with your reply." More than once this policy has alerted a friend or colleague to the fact that their system has been infected with a virus.

Phishers send their e-mails to hundreds of thousands of potential victims; they only need a few people to fall for the scam to make it worth their while. A typical phishing e-mail might look like it came from your bank or a credit card company; the message will say something like: "During our regular verification of accounts, we couldn't verify your information. Please click here to update and verify your information." Or it might be a little more threatening, with a message such as this: "Your account has been suspended. To reactive your account and to avoid permanent termination, please click here to review and update your information." Some phishers are taking a slightly different approach and sending e-mails claiming to be a bank customer satisfaction survey and promising that if you respond to the survey, you will receive a cash reward.

Never reply to these messages and never click on the links. Legitimate companies don't ask for this type of information via e-mail. Banks don't conduct surveys by e-mail—and even if they did, they wouldn't need to ask for your personal information, they would already know it. But, says cyber security expert Christopher Faulkner, an estimated 20 percent of people who receive phishing e-mails will click on the links and fill out the forms, enabling scammers to gather personal and financial data on thousands of people that can then be sold to other criminals.

Phishing scammers are getting more creative and sophisticated by the day. Recently I received an extraordinarily clever e-mail that was probably a phishing or some other type of scam. The e-mail looked like it was sent through eBay using the service eBay offers which allows members to communicate with one another. The graphics appeared authentic, and the text read (and this is copied directly from the e-mail): "Hello, Hi, I signed up for ebay and I've been an ebay member for about 15 days. So, I'm carrying an "icon" where it says "I am a member since less than 30 days." A few days ago, I managed to sell an item. The guy who bought mine left me a positive feedback. But still, mine's got a "zero" feedback? Why is it that? If I click on my profile, I can see that he left me a feedback. But the feedback counting doesn't go from zero to one. Is it because I'm a member who's been registered for less than 30 days? Regards, Gretta."

My first thought was that she was e-mailing me because she had read my book about selling on eBay. Then a couple of red flags popped up in my head. First, I keep my eBay User ID private. Only a very few people know what it is, and it's not mentioned in my book. Second, the e-mail address the message came to is not linked to my eBay account.

All messages that come through eBay will come in both via regular e-mail and in your My eBay page on the eBay site. So I checked, and this e-mail wasn't there. I forwarded the message to eBay's Trust and Safety Department, and they confirmed it was a fake. But it was so well done that I almost clicked on the "Respond Now" link to give her some advice. And had I done that, who knows what might have happened?

Many phishing scams are easy to spot because of the way the e-mail is formatted or because it's full of spelling and grammar errors. But the scammers are getting more sophisticated and not all scams are immediately obvious. Always stop and think before you download a file or click on a link—be absolutely certain you know what and who you're dealing with. Criminals now know how to utilize the login credentials you enter when connecting to an authentic web site to download unique identifying information such as your first and last name. This data is then used to populate portions of the phishing site, making the phony site look more legitimate and making you feel safer divulging your sensitive information.

A Link May Not Be What It Seems

"Link alteration" involves altering the return address in a web page sent to a consumer to make it go to the hacker's site rather than the legitimate site. This is accomplished by adding the hacker's address before the actual address in any e-mail or page that has a request going back to the original site. Criminals have found that if someone unsuspectingly receives a spoofed e-mail requesting him to "click here to update" his account information and then is redirected to a site that looks exactly like his internet service provider (ISP) or a commercial site like eBay or PayPal, there is a better chance that he will follow through in submitting personal and/or credit information.

Usually, if you hold your cursor over the link without clicking, you can see the actual address of the link and may be able to tell if it's been altered. In any case, never click on links in unsolicited e-mails. If the e-mail looks legitimate enough that you want to check it out, close the e-mail and then go to the site in question through the known legitimate links you always use. If a web site address is unfamiliar, it's probably not real.

Fake Money Order or Shipping Agent Scam

You are most likely to be a target of this scam if you are selling something—usually a car, motorcycle, or other high-dollar item—online. Because it's so common for internet shoppers to also be internet sellers, I'm going to share the details of this so you can be on the alert for it.

It works like this: You put your high-dollar item up for sale. A buyer—who seems normal in every other way, even down to a little price haggling—makes an offer that you're willing to accept. He tells you he's located in another country (he may or may not be where he claims) and asks if you'll accept a money order (or sometimes a cashier's check) as payment. You agree. Then he gives you some pretext for sending the money order in an amount larger than the price of the item. A popular excuse is that he got the money order from an American friend who owed him money but he can't easily cash it in his country, so he wants you to cash it, keep the price of the item, and send the difference to him or his "shipping agent" via Western Union. The story sounds reasonable, and you agree. The money order arrives by an overnight courier service and is followed up by an e-mail reminding you to get to the bank, cash it, and send the excess funds as agreed and perhaps even ship the merchandise, unless it's a vehicle he said his "shipping agent" would pick up. You do what you promised—and you never hear from the buyer again. While you're waiting for his shipping agent to pick up the vehicle or while you're spending the money for the item you shipped, a week or two will pass and you'll get a notice from your bank. The money order has been returned unpaid and marked counterfeit and your account has been charged the amount of the money order plus a service fee.

The numbers might look like this: You agree on a price of $8,000 for whatever it is you're selling. He sends you a money order for $10,000 and asks you to send him $2,000 (less the necessary fees) by Western Union. When the money order comes back as bogus, you're out the Western Union fee of about $100, the bank service fee of $20 or $30, and the $1,900 you sent him. And if you shipped the item, you're out the value of that, too.

A friend of mine recently had a car up for sale on the internet and had a fellow who said he was from Canada try this scam. He sent her the fake money order; when she told him she wanted to wait until it cleared before she sent him any money, he kept calling her, asking if the money order had cleared, and saying he was eager to have his shipping agent come by and get the car. Though she hadn't heard of this particular scam, she was savvy enough to be suspicious—and when the bank notified her that the money order was counterfeit and she relayed that information to the "buyer," he said he couldn't believe it, he'd check it out. She never heard from him again. Though she was fortunate not to get scammed, she also doesn't know how many other qualified buyers she missed by taking the car off the market for a few weeks. And because she wasn't a victim, the local police said they couldn't do anything—no crime had been committed in their jurisdiction.

Because I often write about business and finance issues, I'm on the news release list of the Federal Deposit Insurance Corporation (FDIC), which supervises banks and insures deposits. Almost on a daily basis, I get anywhere from one to five e-mail notices of counterfeit bank checks drawn on banks all over the country. The United States Postal Service intercepts thousands of counterfeit United States postal money orders every year. If you receive a bank check, cashier's check, money order, or similar form of certified funds, don't spend the money until you are absolutely certain the document is real. Just because your bank accepts the deposit doesn't mean you're in the clear. Even if the bank doesn't realize until weeks later that it's bogus, your account can still be charged back.

Other Common Online Threats

In addition to outright fraud, when you're on the internet, you are at risk of becoming a victim of a number of other types of online threats. Let's take a quick look at them.

Hoaxes and chain e-mails. They flood e-mail boxes around the world every day: dire warnings about devastating new computer viruses that no one can stop, malicious software that can steal the computer right off your desk, and Trojans that will destroy your system. Then there are the messages about free money and products (trust me, Bill Gates will *not* send you a check for forwarding an e-mail to everybody in your address book), faulty products, sick and missing children (often ending with the guilt-inducing line of "if this were your child, you'd want everyone to help"), prayers, and a variety of other messages designed to grab you and get you to forward the e-mail to everyone you know.

Virtually all of these messages are hoaxes or chain letters, and the only thing they do is clog up e-mail servers and waste time. They don't automatically infect your system like a virus or a Trojan does, but they are still time-consuming and costly to deal with. Folks at the U.S. Department of Energy's Office of Cyber Security say they spend more time de-bunking hoaxes than handling real virus and Trojan incidents.

How do you recognize a hoax or chain e-mail? First, if it asks you to "send this to everyone you know" or to "every address in your book" or some variant of that statement, it's probably a hoax. No real warning message from any credible source will tell you to do that.

Successful hoaxes include technical sounding language and credibility by association. When hoax writers use jargon that sounds like they know what they're talking about, you may be inclined to believe the message—even if you don't understand it. Credibility by association refers to who sent the warning. If, for example, an e-mail about a technical threat comes from someone with a technological organization—even if that person is the janitor—people tend to believe it. Other hoaxes are "authenticated" by "attorneys" or "doctors" who can't be tracked or identified.

Chain letters have a similar pattern. They typically include a hook, a threat, and a request.

The hook catches your interest: Make money fast! Danger! Virus alert! A child is dying! Protect your pet! These tie into our fear for the survival of our computers or into our sympathy for some poor unfortunate person. The threats either warn you about the terrible things that will happen if you do not maintain the chain or they play on greed or sympathy to get you to pass the message on. The threat may include official or technical language to get you to believe it's real. The request is usually to distribute the e-mail to as many people as possible.

Chain letters rarely have the name and contact information of the original sender, making it impossible to verify their authenticity. Newer

Don't Send This to Anyone

Here's an example of an e-mail hoax/chain letter:

> Just thought I would share this with you, as you know I work in the ticket enforcement division and in the course of my investigation into "fines, their payment methods, and how points are assessed against drivers licenses" we discovered something very interesting.
>
> If You Get A Traffic Ticket,
>
> This has been tried and it works.....
>
> I tried to send this to everyone I know. I know that for a fact this works so if you ever get in this situation, you have an out. We discovered that this procedure works in every state. Read it and try it, you have nothing to lose but the points on your license.
>
> This is how it works:
>
> If you get a speeding ticket or went through a red light or whatever the case may be, and you are going to get points on your license, then there is a method to ensure that you DO NOT get any points.
>
> When you get your fine, send in the check to pay for it and if the fine is say, $79, then make the check out for $82 or some small amount over the fine. The system will then have to send you back a check for the difference, but here is the trick!
>
> ***DO NOT CASH THE REFUND CHECK!!!***
>
> Throw it away!! Points are not assessed to your license until all financial transactions are complete. If you do not cash the check, then the transactions are NOT complete. However, the system has gotten its money and is happy and will not bother you any more. This information came to our attention from a very reliable computer company that sets up the standard database used by each states' DMV.
>
> Good luck and share this with all your friends and other family members, as well!!!

■ ■ ■

Though it sounds like something you might want to try, don't bother—and don't pass it on. Here are the facts:

- Most states assess points against your driving record when you are convicted of a violation, not when you pay the fine.

- States don't always automatically issue a refund for small overpayments. Also, checks may be canceled if they are not cashed in a certain period of time, such as 90 or 180 days.

- Versions of this scheme have been circulating for nearly a decade. If by some remote chance it had ever worked anywhere, surely those authorities have heard about it and fixed the loophole by now.

chain letters may have a name and contact information, but it's for a person who either does not exist or who doesn't have anything to do with the hoax message. Legitimate warnings and solicitations will always have complete contact information from the sender.

Before you forward any e-mail—no matter how believable it sounds—check with an authoritative source to confirm its validity. Some good sites to check are: www.snopes.com; www.symantec.com/avcenter/hoax.html; http://urbanlegends.about.com/; http://hoax busters.ciac.org; and www.truthorfiction.com.

Various forms of malicious code, including viruses, worms, and Trojan horses. Viruses are programs that are loaded onto your computer without your knowledge and run against your wishes. Viruses are not accidents or mistakes; they are designed by programmers for a variety of reasons, from pranks to a desire to inflict serious damage. Some viruses don't do anything malicious; others can wipe out all the data on your hard drive, replicate themselves, and use your system to transmit themselves to other systems. Worms are self-propagating viruses. Viruses attach themselves to other programs; worms are self-contained. A Trojan horse is closely related to a virus, but doesn't attempt to replicate itself. Rather, it performs an undesired but intended action while pretending to do something else. Trojan horses can be disguised as directory listers, archivers, games, and even antivirus software. Never load

Test the Transaction for Fraud

The FBI says that if you can answer yes to any one of the following questions, you could be involved in a fraud or about to be scammed. Immediately stop the transaction, and notify the appropriate authorities. If you have received a check:

- Is the check for an item you sold on the internet, such as a car, boat, jewelry, etc.?
- Is the amount of the check more than the item's selling price?
- Did you receive the check via an overnight delivery service?
- Is the check connected to communicating with someone via e-mail?
- Is the check drawn on a business or individual account that is different from the person buying your item or product?

Other circumstances that indicate potential fraud:

- Have you been informed that you are the winner of a lottery, such as Canadian, Australian, El Gordo, or El Mundo, that you did not enter?
- Have you been instructed to either "wire," "send," or "ship" money, as soon as possible, to a large U.S. city or to another country, such as Canada, England, or Nigeria?
- Have you been asked to pay money to receive a deposit from another country such as Canada, England, or Nigeria?
- Are you receiving pay or a commission for facilitating money transfers through your account?
- Did you respond to an e-mail requesting that you confirm, update, or provide your account information?

software on your computer unless you know and trust the source—and know that the source has sufficient computer savvy to not share a virus, worm, or Trojan horse with you.

Fake order confirmation and/or refund e-mails. The subject line says something like "confirming your order #482760" or "your refund has been processed." The e-mail will usually turn out to be a phishing scam or an ad for drugs, stocks, counterfeit products, or something similar. Usually order confirmation e-mails come in within a few minutes of the time you placed your order and will show the company's name in the sender's address or the subject line. If you haven't placed a recent order or requested a refund, don't even open these messages—just delete them. If you open one accidentally, don't click on any links; close the e-mail and delete it. If it's a legitimate request sent to you in error (and it probably isn't) and you don't reply, the company is simply not going to process the order or the refund and will attempt to contact you again.

Tips for Avoiding Scams and Cons

I've seen some online scams that were so clumsy I would be amazed if anyone fell for them. I've seen others that were really slick and might be easy for even a scam-savvy shopper to get taken by. Keep these tips in mind, and you should be safe:

- *Always check out the seller.* It's easy to create a great-looking web site; be sure the company behind the site is just as great. Use the advice in Chapter 2, and never buy from a merchant that doesn't include a verifiable physical address and telephone number on its web site.

- *Don't download software at the request of a web site.* A common scam is that a web site will ask you to download a program, log off, then log back on, claiming that you'll receive some benefit from doing so. But what could happen is that when you log back in you'll be dialing a for-pay phone number and racking up huge bills. Or the program will tell your computer to make direct calls to expensive international numbers. You may not realize what's happened until you get your phone bill.

- *Never respond to spam.* I've said that already; it's worth saying again.
- *Be wary of free trials.* Typically when you sign up for a free trial of anything, you're asked to provide your credit card information so the supplier can begin billing you at the end of the free period if you don't cancel the service. The offer could be legitimate—or you could be serving up your credit card data to a scam artist. Before signing up for a free trial, be absolutely certain you know who you're dealing with. A good guideline is to only accept these offers from well-known, reputable companies.
- *Stay away from "make money" offers.* This includes work-at-home deals and pyramid schemes.
- *Don't give out unnecessary personal information.* This is something else worth repeating; tell merchants what they need to know to complete the sale, and nothing else.
- *If you receive an unsolicited e-mail that asks you, either directly or through a web site, for personal financial or identity information, such as your Social Security number, passwords, or other identifiers, be cautious and suspicious.*
- *If you need to update your information online, use the normal process you've used in the past or open a new browser window and type in the web site address of the legitimate company's account maintenance page.*
- *Always report fraudulent or suspicious e-mail to your ISP.* Reporting instances of spoof web sites will help get these bogus web sites shut down before they can do any more harm. You should also forward it to spam@uce.gov and to the company, bank, or organization impersonated in the e-mail. Most organizations have information on their web sites about where to report problems. Two of the most popular targets of e-mail spoofs are eBay and PayPal users. If you receive an e-mail telling you that you need to update your eBay or PayPal account information, forward the message to spoof@ebay.com or spoof@paypal.com (whichever is appropriate) and delete the message. To confirm that there is

nothing wrong with your account, log into the site through the main address and check on your account information that way.

- *When visiting a web site, take note of the header address that displays in the address box of your browser.* Most legitimate sites have a relatively short internet address that usually depicts the business name followed by ".com" or possibly ".org" or, if it's an overseas address, by a two-letter country code. Spoof sites are more likely to have an excessively long string of characters in the header, with the legitimate business name somewhere in the string or possibly not there at all.

When the Worst Happens and You Are a Victim of Fraud

If you suspect you have been a victim of a scam, the first thing is to go back to the company or individual involved. Gather all of the information about the transaction, including details of the product, the payment, why you think you've been wronged, and what you think would be a good resolution. Get on the phone and call the company (or the seller, if it's an individual) and ask to speak to someone who has the authority to deal with a customer complaint. Stay calm, and speak in a friendly but professional tone. There's always a chance that the situation is an innocent mistake that can be easily rectified, and you'll find people more willing to help you if you're pleasant. Take notes, including the date and time of the call, the names of everyone you speak to, and the results of the conversation. If someone promises to take action, ask when you can expect to see the results and make a note to follow up on that date if necessary. Follow up with an e-mail confirming the details of the call and your understanding of what is going to happen next.

If it turns out that the problem is not fraud but just a mistake, this should take care of it. But if you can't reach the merchant by phone, if you don't get an acceptable response to your call, or if you believe the company has committed intentional fraud rather than being guilty of innocent incompetence, make a formal complaint to the company by mail—regular old snail mail, not e-mail. Keep a copy of your letter, and send it by certified mail, return receipt requested. Address the letter to the president of the company. Often, companies list the names of their officers on their web sites, or you may be able to find that information in the database of the state's division of businesses and corporations. In your letter, describe the situation (as you did over the phone), state what you want to happen, and give the company a reasonable length of time (10 business days or 14 calendar days) to respond. Send a copy to the consumer protection agency in your state and in the state where the company is located, your state attorney general, and any other appropriate consumer organizations.

In most cases, this will get the action you want. If it doesn't, use your copy of the letter to take your complaint to the next level. If you paid by credit card, dispute the charge with your credit card company. Use the basic steps described in Chapter 9 for handling a billing dispute.

If you didn't pay by credit card, if your credit card company won't help, or even if you got your money back but you want to help keep others from becoming victims of the same scam, you should file complaints with as many consumer agencies as you can find.

There are two types of consumer agencies: private and public. Private agencies don't have any legal enforcement clout, but they can exert pressure on the company to resolve your complaint. Public, or government, agencies can take legal steps if your complaint falls within their jurisdictions.

Most agencies will accept complaints online these days, and it's easy to do. As you did before you wrote your letter, get all your information together before you file your complaint. Take the time to compose a summary of the situation in your word processor ahead of time; proofread and spell check the document; then you can just copy and paste that text into the comments space online complaint form. Private consumer agencies include: The Better Business Bureau Online (www.bbb online.org); National Fraud Information Center (www.fraud.org); and Netcheck Commerce Bureau (www.netcheck.com).

You might also complain to any appropriate trade or industry associations. Find them by going to a general search engine and typing in the name of the industry and "trade association" or even just "associa-tion" as your search keywords. For example, if you have a problem with a candy company (as a friend of mine did when she ordered a gift that was never shipped), you could search on "candy trade association." You'll get a long list of links that will take you to organizations that represent various aspects of the candy industry.

When it comes to government consumer agencies, your state's department of consumer affairs (or whatever your state calls it—in Florida, it's the Florida Department of Agriculture and Consumer Services, and I have no idea how those two issues got lumped together in one agency) is a good place to start. Go to your state's main web site to locate the consumer protection agency. You should also send your complaint to the same agency in the state where the company operates. In addition to the appropriate consumer agency, notify the state attorney general of your state and of the state where the company is located. You should also file a complaint with the Federal Trade Commission at www.ftc.gov as well as with the FBI's Internet Fraud Complaint Center at www.ifccfbi.gov. Once your official complaints have been filed, go back to the web sites that review companies and post your experience there.

Often the fact that you have filed these complaints will motivate the merchant to take whatever steps are necessary to satisfy you and get you to withdraw your complaint. However, if all else fails and the dollar value makes additional effort worthwhile, consider suing. If the company (or other party) is in your area, you can take it to small claims court without an attorney. If the amount exceeds the small claims court limit (which is typically between $3,000 and $7,500) in your state, consult with an attorney for advice on your options.

If you have been tricked by a phishing scam into giving personal information to an unknown source, respond as though you have been a victim of identity theft. Immediately check your credit report, put fraud alerts on your credit files, and file a police report—even though you might be embarrassed to admit that you fell for a scam.

Part III

Special Categories Require Special Strategies

Buying High-Priced Merchandise Online

MANY ONLINE SHOPPERS RESTRICT THEIR CYBER-PURCHASES to lower-priced items on the premise that if something goes wrong they won't lose much. But this approach could cause you to miss out on some great deals on higher-priced items. The definition of "high-priced" and the issue of whether or not you should set a price limit on your online purchases are entirely up to you. If you shop carefully and do your homework, the amount you spend—relative to whether you're buying online or in a traditional environment—shouldn't be an issue.

When to Use Escrow

Escrow services can be used for most tangible goods and even some intangible items. Though this is by no means a complete list of when to use an escrow service, if you are buying or selling these or similar items, consider escrow:

- Vehicles
- Construction equipment
- Jewelry
- Antiques
- Original art
- Electronics
- Intellectual property
- Domain names

Knowing who you're buying from becomes even more important when you're looking for high-ticket items. Counterfeit products are all over the internet. Some fake designer named products are priced so low that you know they can't be authentic; others are priced just high enough that you're tempted by what appears to be a good deal; and still others are priced at where you would expect them to be from a reliable source even though they're still fake.

To buy high-end designer items, go to the online merchants you know who deal with these items—Neiman Marcus, Nordstrom, Saks Fifth Avenue, Bloomingdale's, etc. All of these stores have web sites where you can shop and purchase, and you can rely on their quality and service.

For high-priced jewelry, consider shopping online for ideas, but make your purchase from a trusted local merchant. "You have to be very careful buying luxury goods on the internet," says Christopher Faulkner.

"If you can afford to buy a $10,000 watch, you can afford to buy it from your local jeweler to make sure you are getting a legitimate item."

If you decide to go ahead and purchase that high-ticket item online—because you can't find it locally or for whatever reason—do your homework and take steps to protect yourself. At the very least, always pay with a credit card so that you can dispute the charge if the product is not what you were promised.

Escrow for When a Credit Card Isn't Safe Enough

I have already said that credit cards are the safest way to pay for online purchases. While that is generally true, you may want to consider using an escrow service for high-ticket items to give yourself an added layer of protection.

Escrow accounts work like this: You reach an agreement with the seller that includes a description of the merchandise, the sale price, shipping information, and the length of time you have to inspect the merchandise after you receive it. You submit your payment to the escrow agent, using a check, money order, wire transfer, or credit card. The escrow agent verifies the payment and alerts the seller to ship the merchandise and submit tracking information. The escrow agent confirms that the buyer has received the shipment and allows the agreed-on time for the buyer to accept or reject the merchandise. At the end of that time, or sooner if the buyer notifies the escrow agent, the agent pays the seller.

Buyers are protected because the seller isn't paid until you have received, inspected, and accepted what you purchased. Sellers are protected against fraudulent payments. Escrow agents' fees are generally a percentage of the total amount of the transaction, and there may be a minimum amount.

Into Every Great Idea, a Little Fraud Might Fall

Escrow companies have been around for a long time, and they are a great method of safe payment processing for a variety of transactions.

But when a fraudster sees a chance to make money, he'll go for it—so you need to guard against escrow fraud.

The easiest way to avoid becoming a victim of an online escrow fraud is to make sure the escrow company you plan to use is properly licensed. Legitimate online escrow services will usually provide licensing information on their web sites, but you should always take the extra step of verifying that the license is valid by contacting the appropriate agency. Never provide the escrow company with any personal or financial information until you have verified that it is properly licensed.

Buyers and sellers who routinely conduct high-dollar transactions online probably have an escrow service they know and like to use. That's fine, but don't take the other party's word for the legitimacy of the escrow company. Check it out for yourself. If a seller is insistent that you use a particular escrow service, there's an excellent chance he's in on the scam and is trying to direct you to a fraudulent site.

Checking out an escrow company can be a lot of work, but it's a worthwhile investment. Once you find a company you trust that does a good job for you, use it for all your high-ticket transactions. A legitimate seller will not object to your choice of escrow companies.

Carefully review the escrow company's web site and watch for red flags. Avoid escrow company sites that end in .org, .biz, .cc, .info, or .US; most legitimate escrow companies will have a .com site. The site should list a physical address (which you can use to help you verify the license) and telephone number. Call the number and speak to a live person. If a generic voice mail answers, that could be a sign that the company is fraudulent. At the least, it tells you that the company is not particularly sensitive to customer service issues. You don't want to do business with a company you can't reach by phone. In addition to calling, e-mail the company with a question. If you don't get an answer, don't do business with it.

Consider the quality of the site's content—if it's sloppy and inconsistent with spelling and grammar errors, the company could be phony. Of course, many times a scammer will copy a legitimate company's site, so it's possible for a well-done site to be fraudulent. The site may include logos from the Better Business Bureau, VeriSign Secure, Truste, and even the Internet Crime Complaint Center. Don't take these endorsements at face value; verify them with the respective organizations.

Do a search of the company's name on Google or another search engine site. If the company is established and has been operating for any length of time, its web site should come up on your search. If it doesn't, beware. You should also check to see when the site was established and see if that date matches what the company claims on the web site. If the company claims to have been in business for years but the web site has only been registered for a short time, be suspicious. To check on the domain name registration date, use the "whois" tool at any domain name registrar, such as www.networksolutions.com or www.go daddy.com.

You also want to know how the company processes transactions. Only use escrow services that do their own processing; don't use a site that tells you to set up an account with an online payment service. Also, legitimate escrow services do not use person-to-person money transfers (such as Western Union) or have you send your payment to an individual rather than a corporate entity.

While most legitimate escrow companies accept payment via credit card, the fact that a site says it accepts credit cards does not necessarily mean the company is legitimate. It could be a set-up just to steal credit card information.

Chapter 12

Buying Cars Online

WHEN EBAY BREAKS OUT ITS CATEGORIES IN TERMS OF gross merchandise volume—that is, the total value of the goods and services traded on eBay—eBay Motors is at the top. One of the reasons is the simple fact that because cars are typically far more expensive than clothing, collectibles, consumer electronics, and so on, it takes fewer transactions to rack up bigger total dollars. Another is that the category includes automobiles, trucks, boats, parts, accessories, and other vehicles, and that's a lot of high-ticket items. But perhaps the biggest reason is that the buyers and sellers of cars, parts, etc. have enthusiastically embraced the internet as a trading venue because of the tremendous potential market it offers.

Looking for a new car? Use the internet to get all your facts and statistics together before you visit the dealer—or you can even contact the dealer through the internet. If you don't think visiting seven or eight dealers trying to find the car and deal you want is a great way to spend your time, let the internet narrow things down for you and make the entire process more efficient. Looking for a used car? Use the internet to find cars all over the country rather than those just in your local area.

While it's possible to complete a vehicle purchase entirely online (assuming the laws in your state allow it), for most people the best way to approach the transaction is to use the internet to find information or even the specific vehicle you want but complete the sale in person. In fact, Randy Harden, assistant vice president of marketing for CarMax, says that it's rare for the car purchase transaction to be completed entirely online, primarily due to the legal issues related to car sales. He says that many states don't allow dealers to sell a car over the internet and deliver it to the buyer's home. Department of motor vehicle regulations often require that the change of ownership or change of possession occur at the dealer location. These and other regulations are in place to protect consumers from fraudulent dealers, identity theft, and other scams. Of course, if you're buying from an individual rather than a dealer, these restrictions won't apply.

Do Your Homework Online

Use the internet to research the vehicles you're considering. Get all the specs and details so you can compare different makes and models. Great sites for this information on both new and used cars are www.edmunds.com and www.caranddriver.com. For shopping and negotiating a car purchase, check out www.autobytel.com and www.autoweb.com. For general information and a wealth of links to other useful sites, visit www.carbuyingtips.com. There are many, many other sites for car shopping; a search engine can help you find them. Many sites let you enter what you want, and then dealers will bid on your business.

Online Car Shopping Tips

The internet sales consultants at CarMax offer these tips for online car shopping:

1. *Use the internet to research vehicles.*
   - Compare vehicle types, makes, models, features options, and prices.
   - Browse web sites that offer a photo of the car and list all features and options.
   - Look for cars with a no-haggle price that is clearly marked on the web site.
2. *Check on quality.*
   - Be sure that an ASE-certified automotive technician has inspected the car.
   - Carefully review the guarantees and warranties the car seller offers; find out if the car has a warranty and what it covers.
   - Find out if there is a return or exchange policy, and ensure there is a location near you where the car can be returned.
   - Purchase from a retailer that lists its own inventory online and stands behind the quality of its vehicles.
3. *Evaluate the car in person.*
   - Assess the car in person before you buy, including test-driving the vehicle.
   - Run a title check on the car by using AutoCheck (www.autocheck.com, the system CarMax uses) or Carfax (www.carfax.com).
   - Check to make sure the car has the features and options that were listed on the web site.
   - Inspect the vehicle mileage and mechanical condition.
   - Make sure all of your questions have been answered. Don't buy the car if you have vehicle quality concerns or feel you are being rushed.

The great thing about internet car shopping is that you can do your research according to the issues that are most important to you. If you're set on a particular make and model, search on that. If you're on a budget and don't even want to see cars that are more than you want to pay, search by price.

The internet has eliminated much of the mystery of car shopping and practically eliminated many of the car dealer tricks and tactics that made the process of buying a car so miserable. Dealers don't control the information anymore. You can go into the transaction knowing what's a fair price, knowing what the available inventory is, and knowing that you don't have to play games with a salesperson to get the deal you want.

You will find sites that actually sell cars online and use partner dealers to provide delivery of the vehicle. This can save you time and money if you know what you want. I think it's a great idea for new cars, but I still recommend that you not buy a used car without the opportunity to inspect—or reject—the vehicle.

When you're in the market for a used car, you'll find the internet is a more sophisticated version of your local newspaper or trader publication. But if you wouldn't buy a car from a newspaper ad sight unseen, don't do it from a web site.

Paying for Your Car

If you complete your vehicle purchase in person, you can use all the traditional methods of paying—cash, certified funds, financing, leasing, etc. If you are completing the transaction online, use an escrow service (described in the preceding chapter) to make your payment. Chapter 15 discusses borrowing money online.

What to Watch Out For

As with any major purchase, when you buy a car, you should know who you're dealing with. Of course, when you buy a used car from a private party, you take your chances—whether you found that person and car online or in the newspaper or wherever. My first car was a used car I bought from a friend of my father's, and it was a disaster. In less than six months I'd spent more on repairs than the car cost, and it was still breaking down. Years later, I bought a great little used VW bug from a total stranger, and the car served me well (I think either because of or in spite of the huge Georgia Bulldogs decal on the back window). The point is, buying a used car from an individual is somewhat of a gamble, because you don't know what the person might not be telling you, or if there's something wrong that the seller genuinely doesn't know about. When you're buying from a dealer, research that dealer and be sure it's reputable. Find out what sort of guarantees and warranties the dealer offers.

Take the time to have a used car inspected by an independent source who knows what to look for to determine how well the vehicle has been maintained, if it's been in a crash or flood, and other red flags that you should know about. Obtain a vehicle history report through a reputable service that guarantees the information.

Be sure to view the deal from the perspective of both the buyer and seller. Harden puts it this way: "When I am selling my car to somebody, it's in perfect condition and I want top dollar. But when I'm buying, it's somebody else's troubles, and I don't want to pay top dollar for that. Everybody has a different point of view. A creampuff to one person may be a junker to another." Keeping the other person's perspective in mind will help you reach an agreement you'll both be happy with.

If you find a used car in another city, consider how you will arrange to take possession. If you're buying from an individual, you may have to go to wherever the car is and pick it up. Dealers like CarMax will arrange to have the car transferred to a dealer near you.

It Goes Both Ways

Just as you can buy a car over the internet, you can also sell a car that way. Many of the car-selling sites will work with private sellers. Also

check out the auction sites like eBay that have automotive categories. Just be careful when you start negotiating with a buyer because this is a popular place for scammers to operate.

Shopping for Real Estate Online

ECAUSE OF LAWS REGARDING HOW REAL ESTATE TRANS-actions are closed, it's difficult to actually purchase a piece of real property entirely online. Even if that's what you want to do, think about the risks of buying property sight unseen: the structures could need major repairs, the property may not be accessible, you may not be able to get the permits you need to do the improvements you want, and you could end up having to deal with critical deed and title problems. You can, however, make shopping for a new home a lot easier by browsing online first. You can also find rental property, investment property, and even vacation property online.

Finding an Apartment or House to Rent

The last time I looked for an apartment, personal computers were just being introduced and few people knew what the internet was. I pored over apartment guides and the newspaper's classified ads, I spent hours on the phone, and even more driving, looking, and getting lost. It was awful. If you're looking for a house or apartment to rent, take some comfort in the fact that the internet has made the process much easier.

You can search a number of sites for apartments and other rental properties. Check out www.rentnet.com, www.apartments.com, and www.rent.com, or use a search engine to find other sites. Apartment-search sites have much more information than newspaper ads and print directories.

Keep in mind that most apartment-search sites are similar to classified ads in that the property owners pay to have their units listed and provide all the information. Don't be surprised if the listing highlights the positive and downplays the negative. When shopping for an apartment-search site, choose one that includes very detailed listings that describe amenities, shows floor plans, has photos of the units and the complex, and tells something about the neighborhood. The better sites also include a mapping service to help you find complexes and offer e-mail updates so you can be notified immediately if a listing meeting your specific needs becomes available.

An option to renting your own apartment or house is to find a roommate and share that person's home. If you don't know of anyone, check out www.roommates.com. You can search for someone to move into a place you have, a room that you can either rent for yourself or rent out, or a home to share. Shopping for a roommate online is similar to dating online, so even though it can be a very workable solution, exercise caution. Consider using the safety tips for online dating in

Chapter 16, and ask for and check references before you begin sharing a home with anyone.

Shopping Online for a Home to Buy

Trying to find a house to buy without the internet is just as miserable—if not more so—than looking for an apartment. But web sites can give you far more information than print advertisements.

In addition to identifying property for sale, house-finding web sites can give you details about the purchase process, finding financing, taxes, and vital information such as the cost of living, crime rate, transportation, schools, and more. For detailed information on schools in an area where you're shopping for a new home or apartment, check out www.theschoolreport.com.

There are a number of web sites to check out when you're shopping for real estate to buy. At www.realtor.com, you'll find listings *and* real estate agents. Or you can check the web sites of real estate companies or the "for sale by owner" sites.

Jerry and Irene Stoffer, Realtors® with RE/MAX (www.orlandoreal estate.com), tell me that the internet is a great place to start looking for a new home. You can get a good sense of what's available in the market and in your price range before you head out to actually look at property, so you can save time and avoid the disappointment of looking at listings you can't afford. Keep in mind that the same sort of poetic license that sellers have taken for years in their newspaper ads will also appear online. Irene says, "If the remarks read 'fixer upper,' you can pretty well count on the house being a real dog. If it says 'needs TLC,' you can predict the condition will be bad."

In addition to looking for property, you can also look for a real estate agent or broker online. Finding the right real estate agent is as important as finding the right doctor, attorney, or CPA. Remember, this is the person who is going to help you find and negotiate the deal on a home you'll probably be living in for years. Choose an agent with a track record and references you can check.

Buying Real Estate Through Online Auctions

For most things that you buy through an online auction, your bid is a binding contract. Real estate is an exception. Online auction sites such as eBay, Yahoo!, Bidz.com, and others are not licensed auction houses that are qualified to sell real estate. Rather, they are a place where sellers can advertise their property and connect with potential buyers. After the auction closes, the seller and the winning bidder get together and work out the details with a contract that conforms to the laws of the state where the property is located.

   If you're going to shop for real estate through online auctions, first study the rules of the site regarding such sales so you know exactly what you are obligating yourself for if you place a bid.

Timeshares and Other Vacation Rentals

A timeshare is the right to use a vacation property for a specific time period. Timeshare ownership can be deeded, leased, or licensed. Most timeshare ownerships are either deeded or leased for a specific number of years. A deeded timeshare is like any other real estate purchase in that you own the timeshare outright forever; you can rent out your week, sell it, or will it to your heirs. A leased timeshare is similar, except rather than owning the property forever, you have the right to use it for a specific week each year for a specific number of years, typically ranging from 20 to 99 years. When the lease ends, the right to use the property terminates and usually returns to the selling resort. A licensing agreement commonly involves membership in a vacation club.

   If you've ever been to a timeshare sales presentation and have an idea of the initial cost of a timeshare purchase, you'll be pleasantly surprised at the prices in the timeshare resale market. When you buy directly from a resort, the price you pay includes all the administrative and marketing costs associated with the sale of the property. When you buy on the resale market, you are paying closer to the true fair market value of the property, often 30 to 50 percent off the original price. You'll also find plenty of motivated sellers who just want to be rid of their units for whatever reason.

You can buy timeshares and vacation rentals online through agencies that specialize in these types of real estate products. Just type "timeshare resales" in your search engine, and you'll be overwhelmed with the results. Be sure to study each site carefully, understand what's being offered, and do your homework before making a purchase. You can also buy timeshares and vacation rentals through online auctions. The process that you'll use to complete the sale will depend on the type of ownership and local regulations.

Chapter 14

Buying Travel Services Online

T RAVEL IS ONE OF THE MOST POPULAR SERVICES PUR-chased online. As in the real world, you can buy your travel online either direct from the service provider or through an agency. In either case, when you're online you'll have no human interaction, but if you know what you want and don't need advice, that won't matter. If you don't have the time or patience to do a lot of online research and comparison shopping, use a local travel agent—someone you can talk to and get to know, and who can get to know you and your preferences. It might cost a little more, but it will be worth it.

You might consider the internet as a good substitute for a travel guidebook, but experts advise using both. Online, you'll find the web sites for hotels, attractions, and transportation; these sites are electronic brochures designed to promote the facility, and the content is naturally biased. A guidebook gives you a more objective evaluation of those hotels, attractions, and restaurants. Compare the online marketing material with the guidebook review; if there's a tremendous disparity, make your plans with great caution.

Before You Buy

Before you purchase an airline ticket or other travel services on a web site, check the site's security and privacy policy. You should also browse around the site to make sure it's user-friendly and you're comfortable with how it works.

When shopping for flights on the internet, pay attention to all the details. Is the flight nonstop? Is it direct with stops—you don't have to change planes, but the plane will stop enroute? Do you have to change planes, and if so, how long is your layover? Are there any restrictions and what are the cancellation fees? Check the airline's on-time record and also the on-time record for the particular flights you're considering.

You should also find out if there are any time limits between booking, paying for, and using the ticket. Airlines that post last-minute bargains usually have restrictions on the tickets. That's not necessarily bad and the package may still work for you, but you want to know what those restrictions are and be sure you can still get the travel service you want.

When checking prices online, find out if the quoted price includes additional mandatory costs such as taxes, passenger facility charges, ticket processing charges, and fuel surcharges. The basic fare might be a great deal—but the bottom line could be far more than you expected.

Find out if your airline ticket, hotel reservation, or other travel purchase is refundable and/or transferable. Often online specials are not.

Again, this is not necessarily bad, but you want to know if you're risking losing your money if you can't take the trip for any reason.

Keep in mind that the internet is a great way to find unconventional lodgings, such as bed and breakfasts, cottages, cabins, houseboats, and individuals' homes. Do a general search on "vacation rentals," and you'll find hundreds of sites that will let you avoid staying in a traditional hotel or motel.

As with any online merchant, know who you're dealing with when buying travel services. Look for a physical address and telephone number, and verify that information. Check the merchant's reputation, look for industry affiliations, and be sure the agency behind the site is appropriately licensed.

Discount Travel Sites Can Mean Big Savings

If you're a bargain hunter, you'll want to check out the various discount travel sites before you take your next trip. You can find great deals on hotels, airline tickets, cruises, rental cars, and other destination services. Be sure to check out the terms of each site, and get familiar with the various symbols and codes. For example, an asterisk (*) or a plus sign (+) typically means that the price is subject to additional charges, and you want to find out exactly what those charges are before you book your reservation.

I personally prefer Travelocity, but check several discount travel sites to get the best deal. Travelocity (www.travelocity.com), Orbitz (www.orbitz.com), SmarterTravel.com (www.smartertravel.com), and Expedia.com (www.expedia.com) all offer a wide range of travel services and packages. If you just need a hotel room, you might also want to visit Hotel Discounts (www.hoteldiscounts.com).

Going Straight to the Source

Instead of going through an agency site, discount or otherwise, you can also go directly to the airline, hotel, or car rental company's web sites.

Other Valuable Travel Information Sites

Here is a selection of web sites that you may want to check out before your trip:

- *U.S. Department of State*, www.state.gov. Get information about passports and visas; travel warnings, consular information sheets, and public announcements; and details on crisis awareness and preparedness.

- *Centers for Disease Control Travelers' Health page*, www.cdc.gov/travel. Contains health information for specific destinations; vaccination information; dealing with illness or injury abroad; and travel health warnings and notices.

- *U.S. Customs and Border Protection*, www.cbp.gov. Find out what you can bring back from foreign countries and what's involved in getting your items cleared through customs.

- *U.S. Department of Transportation*, www.dot.gov. Click on "citizen resources" for a wide range of information about travel and transportation services in the United States.

- *Travel Guard International*, www.travelguard.com. Insurance that covers vacation and trip cancellation, travel interruptions and delays, emergency medical and health expenses, lost baggage, and more. You can purchase travel insurance through your travel agent or contact providers such as Travel Guard directly.

The deal you get may or may not be better. Or you might use the web sites to gather information and make your plans, then call a toll-free number to actually make reservations. That way you'll have some human interaction and probably a higher level of customer service. When my husband and I were making plans for a trip to Boston with another couple, the four of us crowded around a computer. We found flights that were okay in terms of schedule (not great, but we could live with it) at a pretty decent fare. We decided to call the airline to make the reservation, and the agent we spoke with told us about a flight that wasn't showing up on the airline's web site that was more convenient for us at an even better fare.

A friend of mine who is a white-knuckled flyer likes to have an aisle seat near the front of the plane. He prefers to make flight reservations from the sites that allow you to see the available seats and make a seat selection at the time you purchase your ticket. When he needs to fly on an airline that doesn't show seat availability online, he calls, finds out what's available, then immediately books his tickets online to get the lower internet fare.

Drawbacks of Internet Travel Shopping

If you're accustomed to doing your own travel research and making your own arrangements, you'll find the internet a powerful and convenient tool for making travel related purchases. But if you don't know where to look and what to ask, you'll end up frustrated and wasting time. A web site can only answer the questions you ask, and the only questions it will ask you are related to dates, times, price ranges, and other structured specifics. A human can engage in an interactive relationship and gather information from you that can enhance your travel plans.

Keep in mind that just because a site says a price is discounted doesn't necessarily mean it's the lowest price available or even that it's really discounted. That's why you have to shop around and know what the rates normally are. And speaking of discounts, not all web sites are capable of dealing with senior and AAA discounts. If you're entitled to these or other discounts, you may need to call to make sure you get them.

Finally, remember that it's great when all goes according to plan. But if things go wrong, you may have a hard time getting an online travel agency to help, especially if you don't even know where the agency is located.

Other Things You Can Buy Online

IN ADDITION TO THE ITEMS I'VE ALREADY DISCUSSED, there are a host of other things you can buy online.

All Kinds of Entertainment

You can purchase virtually all kinds of entertainment, from books to music to movies to event tickets, online. One of the most well-known web sites is Amazon.com, which started as an online bookseller and now, in addition to books, offers just about everything from sporting goods to appliances to food. The major chain bookstores all have web sites for online shopping as well.

If you're looking for tickets to a concert, play, sporting event, or other special event, the ads for the event should include ticket buying information and tell you what online agency to contact. Some popular event ticket sites include Ticketmaster, TicketsNow, and TicketLiquidator. Use caution when buying event tickets through online auctions or through any venue not endorsed by the event sponsor; if the ticket is bogus or doesn't arrive on time, you may not have any recourse.

The Internet Is a Virtual Drug Store

It's possible to save a tremendous amount of money buying prescription medication online, but you need to be very careful. Some web sites sell medicines that may not be safe to use and could put your health at risk. But if you buy from a legitimate online pharmacy, you could have a convenient, private way to have your medications delivered to your door and save money in the process. If you have a prescription drug plan, find out if it has an online pharmacy feature.

In any case, make sure any web site where you buy drugs is a U.S. state-licensed pharmacy. Your state's board of pharmacy can tell you if a web site is a state-licensed pharmacy in good standing.

Find Your Pharmacy Board

Locate your state's board of pharmacy through the National Association of Boards of Pharmacy (NABP) at www.nabp.net. The NABP has established the Verified Internet Pharmacy Practice Sites (VIPPS) program with a seal of approval that identifies those online pharmacy sites that are appropriately licensed, are legitimately operating via the internet, and have successfully completed a rigorous criteria review and inspection.

In addition to being state licensed, a safe pharmacy web site should have a licensed pharmacist to answer your questions, require a prescription from your doctor or other licensed health-care professional, and have a way for you to talk to a person if you have questions or problems.

The reality is that some web sites that sell medicine aren't state-licensed pharmacies and may not even be pharmacies at all; they may give a diagnosis that is not correct, sell medicine that is not right for you or your condition, and won't protect your personal information. Some of the medicines sold online are fake; may be too strong or too weak; may have dangerous ingredients; may be expired; aren't FDA-approved; aren't manufactured using safe standards; aren't labeled, stored, or shipped correctly; and may not be safe to use with the other medicines or products you use. It's not known how many people have been harmed from drugs purchased over the internet. However, the sale of unapproved drugs and the illegal sale of approved drugs over the internet poses a serious public health risk.

For example, in one case a man purchased Viagra from a web site and took it without an examination by a health-care professional. He had a family history of heart disease and died after taking the drug. There have been other cases where people chose the internet for treatment to avoid seeing a doctor or other health-care professional. The result can be taking inappropriate and maybe dangerous drugs or purchasing counterfeit or subpotent drugs. Always talk with your doctor and have a physical exam before you get any new medicine for the first time. And never buy prescription drugs from a web site that does not require you to provide a prescription.

Pet Medications

There's a television ad for pet medications that drives me nuts. It talks about getting your pet's heartworm preventative and other medications online and saving a trip to the vet in addition to saving money. What the ad doesn't tell you is that, while there are many online sources for veterinary medications, you must have a prescription to get them and *that* usually requires a trip to the vet. Also, it's important for your pet to see a veterinarian at least once a year for a general checkup and vaccinations. If you want to order heartworm preventative and flea control items from an online source, just ask your vet to write a prescription—but don't skip the exam.

Beyond pet medications, there is a wide range of really cool things you can get online for your pets. If you dote on your "furbabies" like I do, you'll want to browse around the specialty pet supply stores for all the things you didn't even know about but once you see can't live without. One of my favorite pet toy sites is DogToys.com (www.dog toys.com), and I shop both online and in the brick-and-mortar stores of the Petsmart chain (www.petsmart.com). If your pet is on a special diet, you may find it more convenient and perhaps even less expensive to buy the food online; check with the manufacturer to find out how to order.

Groceries and Gourmet Foods

It's possible to do much of your routine grocery shopping online. Net Grocer (www.netgrocer.com) ships groceries to all 50 states, to APO and FPO addresses, and to diplomatic pouch zip codes—making it a convenient way to have your own groceries delivered and to send food and other items to members of the armed forces or diplomatic corps. Some local supermarkets may also offer you the option of online shopping. Before you use an online grocery service, find out how it delivers and what the charges are. Check to see what kind of food it carries, how competitive the prices are, and if it accepts coupons. Also find out what the return policy is.

The internet also offers you opportunities to find and buy edible items beyond your everyday groceries. For gourmet food, exotic foods, or just items you're not likely to find in your neighborhood supermarket, shop online. We have some friends who frequently give parties just to share the delicious food they find online—everything ranging from Cajun style meats to specialty ice creams. Before you buy, find out how the foods are shipped and how foods that need refrigeration are kept cold. Also determine what the shipping charges are. And, of course, be sure you understand the return policy; it should be a no-questions-asked, satisfaction-guaranteed policy.

If you're looking for a particular item, do a search on that product to locate sources. For recipes, links to sites selling fine foods and specialty items, gourmet travel packages, and more, check out www.epicurious.com.

What's Cooking?

The internet is a great source for recipes and cooking tips, and most of them are free. When you're looking for a new recipe, just type the name of what you want to cook and the word "recipe" into a search engine. Some recipe web sites, like Allrecipes.com (www.allrecipes.com), allow users to rank and comment on recipes. For easy-to-prepare dishes, check out Busy Moms Recipes (www.busymomsrecipes.com).

Pieces and Parts

The internet is a great place to find pieces and parts of products, such as remotes for various electronic gadgets, paper trays for printers and copiers, lids or bases for various items, and other parts that can save you having to replacing the entire product. My neighbor lost the remote for her garage door opener; she called the local dealer and got a quote for replacing it, then she did an internet search and found exactly the same item online for half the price. You can also find things like pieces of discontinued china and silver patterns online. Start with a general search on your favorite search engine, then refine as necessary.

Gift Giving Online

The internet has made gift giving easier than ever. All you have to do is pick the gift out, tell the company where to send it, and pay for it—it will arrived wrapped with a personal gift card, and you never had to set foot in a store.

Many general merchandise web sites are set up to accommodate gift giving in the checkout process; others may require special instructions. And then there are sites dedicated to gift giving, such as www.redenve lope.com, www.gifts.com, and www.mypersonalshopper.com.

Many sites have built-in tools that let you categorize gifts by age, occasion, or relationship. Sites with "wish list" tools let the gift recipients show you what they want, and you can decide which items on their wish lists to buy—it's the high-tech, contemporary version of a child's letter to Santa.

Many of the gift sites offer a "thank-you card" service, where recipients can go online to send the giver an acknowledgement. Some actually include a thank-you card in the package for the recipient to sign and mail. It's wonderful when the people you buy gifts for acknowledge them promptly—but if they don't, you should contact them and ask if the gift arrived in good condition. If there's a problem, you want to address it with the merchant immediately.

The Pros and Cons of Online Gift Registries

Online gift registries make it easy to find and send that wedding or baby gift. The biggest drawback is the risk to the gift recipients. Many wedding, baby, and other gift registries make the registrant's addresses publicly available or will give that information to anyone who asks. The danger here is that thieves can easily figure out when a house is likely to be unoccupied—and filled with gifts. Only use online and offline gift registries that keep your address private.

What If They Don't Like It?

Before ordering an online gift, find out what the company's return policy is and be sure it's acceptable. If you're choosing an item the recipient has selected from a registry, the chances of a return are minimal. But if it's a gift you picked out, there's always the possibly the recipient won't like it, can't use it, or already has it. Also, be sure you know the company's policy on what will happen if the merchandise arrives damaged.

Buying and Selling Gift Cards

Gift cards seem like the perfect gift idea: they are easy to purchase, wrap, and ship, and recipients can just buy what they want. But the "gift that can't go wrong" often does. The recipient might not shop in that store, either because he doesn't like it or it just isn't convenient, she may not like the restaurant the card is for, or there might be an assortment of other reasons why a card doesn't get used. Those cards used to just sit in drawers. Today, many of them are being sold on the internet.

First, let's talk about buying new gift cards online. Most retailers that have web sites and offer gift cards allow you to purchase gift cards online. You can have the card sent to you so you can give it personally, you can have the card sent directly to the recipient, or some merchants offer an electronic gift card option that sends the "card" by e-mail for the recipient to use for online purchases.

You can buy a gift card from a specific merchant or a universally accepted card through a financial institution. All major credit cards— MasterCard, Visa, American Express, Discover—offer various types of gift cards that can be used wherever their credit cards are accepted. Retailer-issued gift cards and bank-issued cards are not the same product. Retailer-issued gift cards are a loyalty product designed to increase sales at that particular merchant. Bank-issued cards are payment products that are generally accepted in lieu of credit cards and may have additional features such as lost-card replacement. Bank-issued cards may also have activation or other fees, so be sure to check that out before you buy. Both bank and retailer-issued gift cards are good ideas and serve their respective purposes—just know what you're buying.

Whether you're buying a gift card online or in a brick-and-mortar store, keep these points in mind:

- *Does the recipient use the merchant?* That you shouldn't give a gift card for a steakhouse to a vegetarian seems obvious, but take the time to find what stores and restaurants the recipient prefers before you buy the card. You may not see much difference between Home Depot and Lowe's, but some people do—so don't give a Lowe's gift card to someone who prefers Home Depot. If you're not sure and don't want to ask, consider a universally accepted gift card.

- *Is the merchant conveniently located?* Be sure it will be convenient for the recipient to use the gift card. Not every store is located in every community. If you're sending gift cards out of your area, be sure they are for stores and restaurants near the recipients.
- *Is the amount in proportion to the anticipated purchase?* Don't force the recipient to have to use her own money to make a purchase with the gift you sent. For example, a $25 gift card to an upscale restaurant where dinners average $100 and up per person doesn't make much sense. But a $25 gift card to a bookstore or discount department store can be very useful.
- *What are the terms of the card?* Check to see if the card has an expiration date or if there are fees involved. For example, some cards have what is called dormancy fees that kick in after a period of time (typically six months or a year) that reduce the value of the card by several dollars a month. If the recipient doesn't use the card, the value can literally evaporate. If the merchant charges dormancy fees on gift cards and you want to buy the card anyway, be sure you tell the recipient about the fees so she knows to use the card promptly.
- *Is the retailer established and solvent?* Buying from a large, established merchant reduces the risk that the store could go out of business before the card is used.

For useful tips and news about gift cards, visit www.gift-card-guide .com.

Now let's talk about the relatively new concept of an after market for gift cards that have previously gone unredeemed. Total gift card sales top $65 billion a year, and an estimated 12 to 14 percent of those cards are never "spent." A number of creative entrepreneurs have set up web sites where those cards can be bought, sold, and traded. Typically on these sites the cards sell at a discount off their face value and the sellers pay a small transaction fee. But if you receive a $100 gift card you're not going to use and you can get $90 or even $95 for it, you're probably going to be happy. And if you can buy a gift card for a merchant you like for 5 or 10 percent off the face value, you're going to be happy, too.

Shop and Save for College at the Same Time

You can let your online purchases fund a college savings plan through Upromise (www.upromise.com). One of my friends says she estimates that she does at least half of her shopping online, and when she does it through her Upromise account, a portion of what she spends is deposited in her niece's college savings account.

While this seems like a win-win situation, there are some issues you need to be aware of.

A key issue to keep in mind is that there's no way to be sure that the gift cards are actually worth their advertised value. Some trading site operators have tried to build systems that allow them to confirm the value of a card, but buying gift cards from other than the original seller is a gamble. It's possible that the terms of the card include dormancy fees and if so, the card could be worth far less than its original value simply because it hasn't been used. Also, the cards could be fake, stolen, or used to launder money. Even so, the consumer demand for these after market sales and trading web sites is likely to continue to grow.

If you want to investigate buying, selling, or trading gift cards online, some of the sites that offer these services include: CardAvenue.com (www.cardavenue.com), GiftCardBuyBack.com (www.giftcardbuyback.com), GiftCardsAgain.com (www.giftcardsagain.com), and CertificateSwap.com (www.certificateswap.com). You can also find gift cards for sale on auction sites such as eBay. Just keep in mind that the terms and conditions of how the transactions are conducted vary on each web site, so do your homework.

Online Financial Services

You can research and actually complete a wide range of financial services transactions online, including banking, loans, life insurance, and stock trading. Most of the consumer information web sites will have sections devoted to online financial services, with advice, research, rankings, and links.

There are plenty of legitimate online lenders who are competing for your business. The key to successful borrowing is to give yourself enough time to shop and consider all your options. Check out several online lenders, and compare what they have to offer with local sources. Some online lending sources to research include: E-Loan (www.eloan.com), Quicken Loans (www.quickenloans.com), Lending Tree (www.lendingtree.com), and for car loans, Capital One Auto Finance (www.capitaloneautofinance.com). If you're financing a major purchase—such as a house or car—be sure to research the funding sources available through the broker or salesperson. Before you take out any loan, whether online or not, spend some time browsing around www.bankrate.com. This is a great site with information about rates and plenty of expert financial advice.

It makes sense that a financial site will ask you for personal information if you're opening an account, applying for a loan, or conducting other online financial business. Before you provide the information, be sure the site is secure and that you are indeed on the site you think you are.

InvestorGuide.com (www.investorguide.com) has an almost overwhelming amount of information about investing and finance, including a list of online brokers so you can compare their offerings. The site is big and a little tricky to navigate; it's easiest if you go to the site map and move around from there.

I've already told you to never buy anything that is pitched to you through spam e-mail. This is especially true for stock tips. The only people who make money on e-mail stock tips are the scammers who send them out. They're usually doing something called "pump and dump," where they artificially pump up the price of an obscure, thinly-traded stock, then dump the shares they own, which drives the stock back down. If you're tempted to invest in one of these "hot" tips, take the time to visit www.spamstocktracker.com. This is a site created by Joshua Cyr, who decided to track what would happen if he purchased 1,000 shares of every stock for which he received a hot tip via spam e-mail. He didn't spend any money on this experiment; he did what's called paper trading, which is simulated stock trading. As I write this, he's "lost" almost half of the money he "invested" in more than 35 different stocks.

You can definitely buy stock and other securities through online brokerages. You can subscribe to legitimate free and for-pay online investment newsletters to help guide your decisions. But when it comes to so-called hot stock tips that you receive through unsolicited e-mail, just hit the delete key. Only take investment advice when you initiate the contact from a source you know and trust.

When it comes to buying insurance, you also have a number of online options. However, unless you really understand the complexities of insurance, you may want to use a local agent who can get to know you and determine what coverage you need. For example, you can get a lot of quotes for various insurance products (automobile, term life, homeowners, renters, health, etc.) at www.insweb.com. But when you ask for a car insurance quote online, you're asked if you want limited, standard, or above average coverage; if you don't know what those phrases mean, you won't know what to buy. A good insurance agent can help you figure out how much coverage you need and work with you on ways to keep your premiums affordable.

Business Supplies

If you have a business, online shopping can help you find great suppliers as well as save you time and money. Purchasing managers used to be limited to their local areas for suppliers, but the internet has made it possible for even small companies to shop on a worldwide basis.

To find suppliers, check out sites designed for procurement professionals, such as Thomas Net (www.thomasnet.com), Reed Link (www.reedlink.com), and Kelly Search (www.kellysearch.com). These sites can connect you with literally millions of suppliers around the world. You can also use the internet to purchase through a reverse auction, where you post what you want and companies submit offers.

Of course, you can save time and money buying online from suppliers close to home. For example, as much as I love wandering through an office supply store checking out all the new gadgets, when I'm short on time and know what I need, I just go online to one of the office supply chains, place my order, and it is delivered the next day. Staples (www.staples.com), OfficeMax (www.officemax.com), and Office Depot (www.officedepot.com) offer free delivery on orders over $50. If you run a business, even a small one, it's easy to spend more than $50 on office supplies. Even if you don't run a business, office supply stores are great resources for school supplies, some household items, and even furniture. Not long ago I was looking for a cabinet for our breakfast room. I had a mental picture of what I wanted and was searching furniture stores without success. Then I decided to check the office supply stores. Staples had exactly what I wanted for about a fourth of what the furniture stores were charging for something in the category that I didn't want—and because it was more than $50, delivery was free.

Because this is a guide for consumers, I'm not going to spend a great deal of time on complex business buying issues. I'm just going to say that if you have a business, no matter how small or large, you should be using the internet to make your procurement system more effective. For more information about professional purchasing, check out *Purchasing* magazine at www.purchasing.com.

More Than Things: Finding Friends, Dates, and Jobs Online

ALTHOUGH IT'S NOT EXACTLY SHOPPING (WELL, MAYBE IN a way it is), the internet can be a great place to meet exciting, interesting people, whether you're looking for friends or romance. I'm starting to lose count of the number of happily married couples I know who met online—and happily single people who meet people to date and socialize with online. Also, my husband and I have a number of friends we met through various online venues such as discussion boards and lists. For example,

I'm a dog lover, and I have several dear friends I initially got to know on breed-specific discussion lists, others I met through faith-based lists, and still others my husband and I got to know on running forums.

Sharing Common Interests

Online discussion boards, forums, and lists are wonderful places to exchange information and ideas with people on specific topics. You'll find discussion boards on Yahoo!, Google, iVillage, and more. Many companies, such as Apple Computers, eBay, Ilford Imaging, Disney, and others sponsor discussion boards for their customers. On a discussion board, you log onto the site and read the postings. On a list, the postings are sent out to subscribers by e-mail, or you can read them online instead. Every board, forum, and list has its own set of rules established by the list owner as well as by the host site. It's a good idea to read the rules and then spend some time monitoring the discussions quietly (in the online world, this is called lurking) before you join in.

The internet is full of people who just enjoy interacting with others online—and a few nut cases who occasionally make things a challenge for everyone. It's a lot like an office, a club, or even a family—and just like in those real world situations, you need to balance what you read with what you know to be true, not accept everything as gospel, and not be shocked at what some people will reveal to virtual strangers.

Just because you join an online group doesn't mean you have to belong to it forever. You may decide you don't like the people or it's just not worth your time. Or you may join for a specific purpose and leave when you no longer have a need to be there. For example, years ago I had a dog with Cushing's disease. I immediately joined a discussion list of people with dogs who had this condition, learned a lot, and was able to give my dog a more informed level of care. For a while after she died, I stayed on the list to offer the same assistance I had received, but eventually I dropped off. My husband is a photographer, and he participates on several discussion boards that revolve around particular products or equipment manufacturers (one is the Ilford Imaging board I mentioned). He and the other participants ask for and receive advice, help each other figure out problems, and share information in a way that would be impossible without the internet.

Keep in mind that whatever you post to a discussion board, forum, list, or any similar site will be public and available to just about anyone to see, so don't put anything private on them. Also, never assume that people are who they say they are or that they really know what they claim to know. Most people on discussion boards are honest and try to be genuinely helpful, but they may sometimes be mistaken about things. And there are always the few who misrepresent themselves for various reasons that could range from harmless pretending to serious

A Different Kind of Internet Love Story

This is a story of faith, love, and hope on the internet. It began, unfortunately, with a tragedy.

On May 27, Mary Kinney—a former Central Florida resident serving as a missionary on the Arizona/Mexico border—posted an e-mail message to a friend in Winter Park. Briefly, she reported that her daughter, Debi, and son-in-law, Jason, had been in a serious car crash in Montana. She said she was en route to the hospital in Billings and asked for prayers.

The friend forwarded the message to everyone she knew who knew Mary, locally and throughout the world. And the prayers began. During the next few days, the friend posted e-mail updates each time she talked with Mary. Debi and Jason had been driving from Florida, where they had been visiting family, back to their home in Seattle when the crash occurred. Sadly, Jason did not survive, and Debi suffered serious brain injuries and was in intensive care.

In a strange town with limited resources, Mary hovered over Debi's bed. It was anguish compounded by geography. I knew that I was not alone in wishing that there was more I could do, but, from here in Florida, prayers were the best I had to offer.

Then I realized I had a unique network that might be of some help. A dog lover, I am on two breed-specific internet mailing lists. I posted a notice to both lists, describing the situation, and asking if there were any members near Billings who could possibly do something. It didn't have to be much, perhaps just someone stopping by the hospital, maybe taking Mary lunch, or even offering her a place to come for a home-cooked meal and a chance to do her laundry.

The response was heartwarming. People on the lists who lived near Billings went to the hospital. One woman drove 45 miles just to give Mary a hug. Another, in the middle of selling her house and moving herself, took the time to visit daily. After reading the notice, a Florida "lister" called her cousin who lives in Billings; he brought a meal and flowers to the hospital. Others not close enough to visit asked if they could send donations, cards, and gifts.

On June 13, Debi was flown by air ambulance to Orlando to undergo rehabilitation at a local hospital. The internet and e-mail continued to play a major role in communication and support, as all of Mary's friends—both long-time and new—were kept up-to-date on Debi's progress through daily postings. Debi's recovery will be a lengthy process, but she and her family won't be going through it alone.

Amid stories of fraud, betrayal, and pornography on the internet, this is a tale of a lot of good-hearted people using that same electronic network to reach out to someone in need.

Connected in cyberspace through their common concern for a young woman many of them have never even met, members of this caring group have forged and strengthened their own mutual bonds. And without thought for recognition or reward, they've clearly demonstrated how the innate goodness of the human race can be enhanced by technology.

It's a lesson worth remembering.

Note: I wrote this article in 1998; it was originally published in the Orlando Sentinel *and later reprinted in* Catholic Digest. *Debi has recovered to the point that she is now able to live on her own, and has returned to Seattle. Mary has returned to her mission work.*

malicious intent. After a while, you will develop a sense of who is real and who isn't—but there will probably always be a con artist who is able to fool you.

Of course, you will meet con artists in any venue—clubs, associations, church, etc. So don't let that prevent you from taking advantage of the opportunity to make online friends who share your interests around the world. And if at any point you decide to meet any of these people face-to-face, just be cautious and use common sense. Apply the advice in the section about online dating.

Online Dating

If you've heard about the internet, you've probably heard about online dating. It wasn't so long ago that advertising for a date was something only "losers" or predators did. Today, people from all walks of life, from blue-collar workers to highly paid professionals, are meeting through online services, and many of those relationships progress to marriage.

A friend of mine who has been meeting men online for years told me how she calmed her father's fears of the process. She pointed out that she didn't want to date men she met through work because she liked to keep her professional relationships professional. She didn't have any hobbies that offered opportunities for meeting men. She didn't go to church. And although she would occasionally get set up on a blind date, it didn't happen often. Her options then, she said, were to hang out in bars or meet men through online dating services—and when you meet a man in a bar, the only thing you can be sure of is that he drinks. You have no way of knowing if he's married or single, dangerous or harmless, or if anything else he says is true. But she figured that when she met a man online, he at least had the wherewithal to own and use a computer. And by exchanging e-mails for a while before meeting him in person, she could get to know enough about him to decide if she even wanted to meet him. My friend's father saw her point—although I'm not sure he ever became truly comfortable with the idea of online dating.

Online dating provides you with a means to expand your social opportunities and gives you a chance to quickly screen out people you're not interested in. The online services let you post a profile and allow you to view other profiles so you can find people who share your interests, goals, and values. Because most people post photos with their profiles, you'll be able to quickly weed out anyone you find physically unacceptable. By reviewing profiles and photos, then exchanging e-mails, you can decide if you want to move to the level of personal contact. A friend of mine who regularly dates men she meets through online services says communication skills are important to her, so she doesn't reply to e-mails that contain a lot of spelling, grammar, and punctuation errors—even though the man's profile might be appealing. She says a poorly written e-mail tells her the man either doesn't know or doesn't care how to write clearly—either way, she's not interested. On the other hand, even though she is strikingly attractive, she doesn't care whether a potential date is extremely good-looking, ordinary, or even homely.

A big advantage of online dating is that everyone who is on the site is interested in meeting someone—and everyone else knows and understands that. If you're single and you've been in a situation where you met someone you found attractive, but you weren't sure of that person's marital or relationship status, or even sexual orientation, you will appreciate this advantage. All of those issues are handled up front without any awkwardness.

There are some free online dating services, but most charge a fee for full access to the site and its programs—typically anywhere from $10 to $50 a month. I did an informal and unscientific poll of the people I know. They all agree that you'll get better results from the sites that charge a fee. The reasons they gave included the fact that the people who are willing to pay a fee are likely to be more serious about finding a partner and less likely to be a liar or cheater, and the willingness to pay a fee demonstrates a minimal level of financial resources. Most of the online dating services offer a free introductory period so you can test the waters before you have to make a financial commitment. Several internet dating sites are listed in the appendix. You should also ask people you know for recommendations.

Staying Safe in Any Environment

Whether you're looking for romance or just making platonic friends online, protect yourself with common sense. Don't give out too much personal information too soon, and if someone pressures you for personal information, end the conversation. Pay attention to your intuition; if the other person is saying things that make you uncomfortable, figure out why you feel that way. For example, if you're getting contradictory details, it might be that you simply misunderstood—or it might be that the person is lying and forgot what he or she said.

After you've exchanged e-mails and perhaps chatted through instant messages, spend some time talking on the phone before you set up a face-to-face meeting. Use a cell phone to protect your privacy; it's still too soon to let the person know where you live.

Your first meeting should be in a public place where other people will be around. Restaurants and coffee shops are usually the best choices. Let someone know where you're going and when, and when you will be home. Have a plan for what that person should do if you don't come home on schedule—and that means if you change your plans, you need to let that person know. You might even consider taking a friend with you—the friend could discretely stay out of sight but be there in case anything goes wrong. Always have your own transportation so you can leave if you feel uncomfortable. If you have to drive or fly to another city for the meeting, make your own hotel reservations and do not tell the other person where you are staying. If you fly, rent a car so you can drive yourself to the hotel and then to the meeting. Make sure someone knows where you are and how to reach you, and that you check in regularly.

If someone asks you to send money so you can meet him or her, don't. In fact, if you are asked for money before you meet or very early in the relationship, be very suspicious.

Never do anything that makes you feel unsure or uncomfortable. If your date is pressuring you about anything or if you feel afraid, end the meeting and leave. If necessary, ask someone else for assistance—you might, for example, ask a restaurant staffer to escort you to your car. Or if

What Does That Mean?

If you're new to online dating and discussion boards, you may not understand the various abbreviations that are frequently used. Here's a list of the most common ones:

AKA: Also known as

ANI: Age not important

ASL: Age/sex/location

ATM: At the moment

AWYR: Awaiting your reply

B4N: Bye for now

BF: Boyfriend

BRB: Be right back

BTU: Back to you

BTW: By the way

CUL: Catch you later

DBF: Divorced black female

DBM: Divorced black male

DOB: Date of birth

DWF: Divorced white female

DWM: Divorced white male

F2F: Face to face

FYI: For your information

GMAB: Give me a break

GOI: Get over it

GSOH: Good sense of humor

GTG: Got to go

H/W/P: Height/weight proportional

HAK: Hugs and kisses

ICBW: I could be wrong

IGTP: I get the point

IM: Instant message

IMHO: In my humble opinion

IMO: In my opinion

ISO: In search of

J/K: Just kidding

KIT: Keep in touch

LDR: Long-distance relationship

LJBF: Let's just be friends

LMAO: Laughing my ass off

LOL: Laughing out loud

LTR: Long-term relationship

MYOB: Mind your own business

N/S: Nonsmoker

NRN: No reply necessary

PDA: Public display of affection

SBF: Single black female

SBM: Single black male

SWF: Single white female

SWM: Single white male

SWNSF: Single white nonsmoking female

SWNSM: Single white nonsmoking male

SYT: See you tonight

TAFN: That's all for now

TTYL: Talk to you later

TYVM: Thank you very much

WLTM: Would like to meet

YOA: Years of age

the situation is really bad, excuse yourself to go to the restroom, then slip out the back door. If you feel that you are in danger, call the police, even if you feel silly doing so. Nobody has ever died of embarrassment, and your safety is more important than your pride or someone else's opinion of you.

Most of the time, these precautions will not be necessary. And taking them doesn't mean there is an unusual risk associated with online dating. The reality is you can meet dangerous people anywhere—your risk of meeting a loser online isn't any greater than if you met at church, at work, in a bar, or anywhere else.

Protect Your Pocketbook

In the next section about finding a job online, I'll explain a payment transfer scam that targets jobs seekers. A similar scam is common on dating sites and other types of chat rooms. There are plenty of honest people just looking for friends and romance online, but be aware that there are still some fraudsters out there.

Here's a true story that illustrates how these scammers work. A woman in South Florida had been chatting online through an instant messenger service several nights a week with a man she met through a dating site. He had an American name and said he was a U.S. citizen working as a geologist and computer engineer in Nigeria. He spent several months building the relationship and getting her to trust him. Then one night, near the end of a long chat, he typed: "can u help me cash money orders baby." He asked if he could send her some money orders and travelers checks that he couldn't cash in Nigeria. He wanted her to deposit them in her bank account and send him the cash through Western Union. She figured the MasterCard travelers checks and the United States Postal Service money orders were safe, so she did as he asked. Once he got her money, she never heard from him again. And eight days later, she learned that the checks were bogus. Her bank told her that she was responsible for repaying the total of the counterfeit checks: $9,200. It said that the fact that its customer was defrauded was "unfortunate," but that "customers are liable for the soundness of checks and other instruments that they deposit."

This woman is a well-educated schoolteacher. She's not stupid; she thought she was doing a friend a favor and didn't realize the risk involved. But she couldn't afford to take a loss of almost $10,000, and it will take her years to recover from the financial damage. She may never recover from the emotional toll.

If anybody ever asks you to deposit checks or money orders and send them cash, don't do it. Period. Even if you're told you can make some easy money in the transaction. Many fraud victims let greed get in the way of their common sense—don't let that happen to you.

The internet is a great way to get to know people you might not otherwise have the opportunity to meet. Take advantage of that—but always, always protect yourself first.

Looking for Jobs Online

As with so many other things, the internet has expanded the opportunities available to job-seekers—but before you start your online job search, know how the process works and what the potential risks are. A great place to start an online job search is a www.job-hunt.org. The site provides a comprehensive listing of useful online job-search resources and services, along with articles for safe and effective job searching.

You've probably heard of the online employment super sites like www.monster.com, www.careerbuilder.com, www.hotjobs.com, and www.careerjournal.com, which can be great resources. But don't stop there. If you're interested in working for a particular company, visit its web site. Most companies will have a link on their home pages to "employment opportunities" (or similar language) that will tell you how to submit an application and may even list current openings.

Many professional associations offer their members the opportunity to post job openings on the association's site. These listings are usually restricted to members and are not always up-to-date, but if you're already a member, they can be worth checking out. You should also research specialized and regional employment sites. The specialized sites focus on a particular employment niche, the regional sites on a designated geographic area. You might also want to consider checking out the sites of recruiters or headhunters—but be sure you understand their fee structure and how they work before you sign up with them.

If you currently have a job and don't want your employer to know you are looking for a new one, be very cautious about posting your resume on online job sites. You really have no way of knowing who is going to see your information. Some job sites offer cloaking functions that can conceal your contact information; consider using those services. Even if you are looking for opportunities at a particular company, keep in mind that it's common for companies to outsource the careers/employment section of their web sites. That means a resume submitted online to a specific company could end up in a larger database that may be searched by all the clients of the firm providing the service.

Employment scams have been around almost as long as jobs have. In the past, con artists had to put forth some effort with their job scams by running ads, having working telephone numbers, and maybe even physical offices. They'd run their scams until they were at risk of getting caught, then move on to another city. Just as the internet has opened doors for job seekers, it's made it easier for criminals who are targeting people when they are often most vulnerable and least able to afford it.

Legitimate employment sites have taken steps to reduce fraud, but con artists have found that online job seekers are a rich source from which they can steal money, bank account numbers, identities, and Social Security numbers with relative ease and low risk. Before you start looking for a job online, understand how these thieves operate and know how to protect yourself.

The Payment Transfer Scam

There are a number of variations of the payment transfer scam, but it basically works like this: The con artist pretends to be an employer and the "job" involves forwarding or wiring money from a personal bank account, a PayPal account, or from a Western Union office to another account or person. These scammers can be very convincing, and they often steal real company names and logos to make themselves look even more legitimate.

The con artist will typically recruit multiple victims and put them through an interview process that seems very credible. The victims are asked to give their bank account numbers for direct deposit of their pay-checks. The con artist then uses that information to access the accounts and steal money, which may be used to purchase goods or may be trans-ferred into other accounts. The final victim in the scam is wired the stolen money (usually an amount under $10,000, so it is less likely to be scrutinized by a bank) and told to keep a percentage of the funds and transfer the remainder to a new account. When the victim participates in the transaction, he unwittingly becomes an accomplice because he has accepted and transferred stolen money. It's possible that the victim could indeed be arrested and prosecuted.

The variations on this scam are limited only by the imaginations of the thieves who perpetrate them. The World Privacy Forum, which has done extensive research into online job scams, reports that a good con artist can ensnare even the most knowledgeable financial professionals in these scams.

How can you protect yourself from this and other scams when look-ing for a job online? Follow these tips:

- Be very cautious when deciding what information to include in an online resume. Not every job site is legitimate, and not every job posting on legitimate sites is real. Know who you're dealing with before you give out personal information. And *never* put your Social Security number on your resume, whether you are posting it online or handing it to someone in person.
- Until you are certain that you are dealing with a legitimate com-pany, give a cell phone rather than your home phone number and use an e-mail account you set up specifically for your job search.
- Before you post a resume or any other information on a job site, read the site's privacy policy carefully and be sure you are com-fortable with what it says.

- Be wary if you are asked for personal or financial information by phone, e-mail, or online. Most employers will not ask for this information until you arrive at their offices for an in-person interview and are given a formal job application.

- Legitimate employers do not ask for the information necessary for direct deposit of paychecks until you have been hired. Also, although many employers prefer that workers accept direct deposit payments, they will usually offer an alternative if you are not comfortable with that process.

- If you are asked to transfer money and retain a portion for payment, you are probably being set up for a scam. Don't do it. And never forward, transfer, or wire money to an employer.

- Watch for red flags that indicate you're dealing with a scammer: requests for bank account numbers and Social Security numbers; requests to "verify identity" with a scan of a drivers' license or other official identification; a contact e-mail address that is not a primary domain (for example, if a representative of a company calling itself General Industries sends e-mail from a Yahoo! or Hotmail address, be suspicious); misspellings and grammatical errors in the ad and in correspondence; ads for jobs that include tasks such as package-forwarding, money transfers, and wiring funds; and the phrase "foreign agent agreement" in the job description or contract.

Part IV

The Future of Online Shopping

Chapter 17

Looking Ahead

WHAT DOES THE FUTURE HOLD FOR ONLINE SHOPPING? THE short answer is: More and better. Online shopping has come an incredibly long way in just the past decade. From slow dial-up connections and web sites that were little more than online billboards, e-commerce has evolved to high-speed connections (for many, anyway) and easy-to-use shopping sites full of information and resources. It's estimated that by the year 2010, internet sales will account for some 12 percent of all retail sales by American firms.

But it hasn't been a smooth road. Remember 1998 and 1999 when ToysRUs.com was overwhelmed by online shoppers? The company was unable meet consumer demand, and countless Christmas gifts didn't arrive on time. We're not quite where we need to be yet. But we're on the way.

The development of affordable, easy-to-use e-commerce solutions has enabled more companies of all sizes to launch internet operations. Consumer confidence in online buying is on the upswing, and it won't be long before a generation of shoppers who never knew a world without e-tailers reaches adulthood.

Expect to see more ease of use, increasingly reliable and efficient technology, and greater choices in e-commerce. Wireless and mobile e-commerce will also very likely increase, with customers placing orders from their cell phones and PDAs. Christopher Faulkner sees people shopping from their handheld devices while commuting and in other away-from-home situations. He believes merchants will anticipate the trend by designing web sites that can be viewed by these devices. He also predicts advances in technologies such as smart cards and biometric identification systems that will help verify identities and reduce the risk of theft and fraud.

While some people will always want to browse in stores and malls, the convenience factor of online shopping will drive increasing numbers to make at least a substantial portion of their purchases over the internet. As technology continues to advance and e-commerce software become more user-friendly and efficient, online shopping will grow. And as virtual communities (people getting together online in common interest groups) grow, the balance of economic power will shift from the manufacturer to the consumer.

Smart companies are already on the e-commerce bandwagon and more will follow. Smart consumers are ready to take advantage of the tremendous range of goods and services available at the touch of their fingers. And it's only going to get better for everyone.

See you online!

Online Shopping Resources

THROUGHOUT THIS BOOK, I HAVE MADE REFERENCES TO various web sites. Here is a consolidated listing of those sites, first in alphabetical order, then organized by category.

Alphabetical List of Web Sites

Able Shoppers, www.ableshoppers.com, specials and coupons.

About Urban Legends and Folklore, http://urbanlegends .about.com, a site that researches and provides details on urban legends, internet hoaxes, and netlore.

Allrecipes.com, www.allrecipes.com, features recipes and allows users to rank and comment on recipes.

AltaVista, www.altavista.com, search engine, shopping, travel, and more.

Amazon.com, www.amazon.com, a retail site selling books, music, and a wide range of other consumer products that allows consumers to review and rank the items it sells.

AnnualCreditReport, www.annualcreditreport.com, a centralized service for consumers to request free annual credit reports.

Apartments.com, www.apartments.com, nationwide apartment search site.

Ask Jeeves, www.askjeeves.com, search engine, shopping, and more.

AuctionBlitz, www.auctionblitz.com, auction sniping software.

AuctionSniper, www.auctionsniper.com, auction sniping software.

Autobytel, Inc., www.autobytel.com, an internet automotive marketing services company offering new and used car pricing and information.

AutoCheck, www.autocheck.com, vehicle history reports for used cars.

AutoWeb, www.autoweb.com, a third-party automotive e-commerce site offering pricing and other information.

Bankrate, www.bankrate.com, online financial rate information.

Better Business Bureau, www.bbb.org, a network of agencies that collects and provides information about companies.

Better Business Bureau Online, www.bbbonline.org, a site of the Better Business Bureau focused on promoting trust and confidence on the internet.

Bidpay, www.bidpay.com, online auction payment service.

Bidville, www.bidville.com, online auction site.

Bidz.com, www.bidz.com, online auction site.

BizRate, www.bizrate.com, consumer feedback site operated by Shopzilla.

Busy Moms Recipes, www.busymomsrecipes.com, easy-to-prepare recipes and monthly newsletter.

Capital One Auto Finance, www.capitaloneautofinance.com, automobile loans.

Car and Driver, www.caranddriver.com, the web site of *Car and Driver* magazine.

CarBuyingTips, www.carbuyingtips.com, advice on car buying, leasing, and avoiding dealer scams.

CardAvenue.com, www.cardavenue.com, buy, sell, and trade gift cards.

Career Journal, www.careerjournal.com, the *Wall Street Journal's* executive career site.

CareerBuilder, www.careerbuilder.com, job search and employment site.

Carfax, www.carfax.com, vehicle history reports for used cars.

Centers for Disease Control Travelers' Health page, www.cdc.gov/travel, information for specific destinations, vaccination information, advice for dealing with injury or illness abroad, and travel health warnings and notices.

CertificateSwap.com, www.certificateswap.com, a gift certificate marketplace that allows consumers to purchase or sell gift certificates.

CNET, www.cnet.com, professional and consumer product reviews and price comparisons for technology-related products.

Complaints.com, www.complaints.com, a database of personal, firsthand, consumer experiences with products and services.

Consumer Action Website, www.consumeraction.gov, consumer information.

Consumer Reports, www.consumerreports.org, the web site for the popular consumer magazine.

Consumerreview.com, www.consumerreview.com, provides reviews, advice, and shopping opportunities for outdoor sporting goods and consumer electronics.

ConsumerSearch, www.consumersearch.com, gathers and analyzes product reviews and offers a list of top-rated products.

ConsumerWorld.org, www.consumerworld.org, a guide of consumer resources.

Cookie Central, www.cookiecentral.com, information and news about cookies.

CoolSavings, www.coolsavings.com, online and printable coupons.

Costco, www.costco.com, Costco Wholesale's online store.

Coupon Cabin, www.couponcabin.com, online coupons and promotional codes.

CouponMountain, www.couponmountain.com, free coupons.

Current Codes, www.currentcodes.com, discount and coupon codes.

Deal Catcher, www.dealcatcher.com, store ads, coupons, specials.

Deal Hunting, www.dealhunting.com, coupons and great deals.

Deal Taker, www.dealtaker.com, coupons and special deals.

Dogpile, www.dogpile.com, general search engine that searches other major search engine sites.

DogToys.com, www.dogtoys.com, pet toys and supplies.

Download.com, www.download.com, offers a wide variety of downloadable software, including free and for-pay spyware removal programs, plus free and trial offers from various software companies.

eBay, Inc., www.ebay.com, worldwide online marketplace where users buy and sell in auction and fixed price formats.

Edmunds.com, Inc., www.edmunds.com, new and used automotive pricing, vehicle reviews, and other information about the automobile purchase process.

eHarmony, www.eharmony.com, online introduction and dating service.

E-Loan, www.eloan.com, mortgage, auto, and personal loans.

Epicurious, www.epicurious.com, features recipes, links to sites selling fine foods and specialty items, gourmet travel packages.

Epinions, www.epinions.com, offers product reviews and recommendations, plus links to merchants.

ePublicEye.com, www.epubliceye.com, a site that allows consumers to rate e-businesses for reliability, privacy, and customer satisfaction.

eSnipe, www.esnipe.com, auction sniping software.

Expedia.com, www.expedia.com, online travel site.

FatWallet, www.fatwallet.com, source for online coupons, bargain shopping, and price comparisons.

FBI's Internet Fraud Complaint Center, www.ifccfbi.gov, a resource for information about internet crimes and a place to file a complaint if you have been a victim.

Federal Deposit Insurance Corporation (FDIC), www.fdic.gov, supervises banks and insures deposits.

Federal Trade Commission, www.ftc.gov, the United States consumer protection agency.

Freecreditreport, www.freecreditreport.com, a commercial site of Experian, a credit reporting agency that offers a free copy of your credit report when you sign up for a trial membership in its monthly credit monitoring service; do not confuse this site with www.annualcreditreport.com, where you can get a no-strings-attached free copy of your credit report.

Froogle, www.froogle.com, Google's shopping site.

GeoCities, www.geocities.com, free and fee-based web hosting (a Yahoo! service).

GeoTrust, www.geotrust.com, digital certificate provider offering online transaction security, identity verification, and trust services.

GetNetWise, www.getnetwise.org, a collaborative effort of a broad-based coalition of companies, public interest organizations, non-profits, and trade associations with information to show internet users how to stay safe and secure online.

Gift Card Guide, www.gift-card-guide.com, information and news about gift cards.

GiftCardBuyBack.com, www.giftcardbuyback.com, buy, sell, and trade gift cards.

GiftCardsAgain.com, www.giftcardsagain.com, buy, sell, and trade gift cards.

Gifts.com, www.gifts.com, gifts.

GoDaddy, www.godaddy.com, domain name registration, transfer, hosting.

Google, www.google.com, search engine, shopping.

Great Expectations, www.great-expectations.com, online introduction and dating service.

Hoaxbusters, http://hoaxbusters.ciac.org/, the U.S. Department of Energy's site on internet hoaxes.

Hot Deals Club, www.hotdealsclub.com, online deals, coupons, promotions.

Hotel Discounts, www.hoteldiscounts.com, discounted hotel accommodations.

Hotjobs, www.hotjobs.com, Yahoo!'s job search site.

InsWeb, www.insweb, online insurance marketplace for automobile, term life, homeowners, renters, and individual health insurance products.

Internet Shopper, www.internetshopper.com, comparison site for products, prices, and merchants.

InvestorGuide.com, www.investorguide.com, information about investing and finance.

iVillage, www.ivillage.com, describes itself as "the internet for women," includes a search engine, discussion boards, and more.

Job-Hunt.org, www.job-hunt.org, online job search guide and resource directory.

Kelly Search, www.kellysearch.com, an industrial product and service search engine featuring a global database of companies.

Lending Tree, www.lendingtree.com, mortgage, auto, and other loans.

LexisNexis, www.lexisnexis.com, subscription-based search engine for legal, news, and business information.

Lycos, www.lycos.com, general search engine, web hosting, blogging, discussion groups, and more.

Match.com, www.match.com, online introduction and dating service.

Monster, www.monster.com, job search and employment site.

My Personal Shopper, www.mypersonalshopper.com, personal shopping service.

My Rebates, www.myrebates.com, find and buy products with rebates, track rebates.

National Association of Boards of Pharmacy (NABP), www.nabp.net, a professional association representing state boards of pharmacy in the United States and certain other countries.

National Association of Realtors, www.realtor.com, information on finding and buying a home, rentals, financing, moving, and more.

National Fraud Information Center, www.fraud.org, information on internet and telemarketing fraud.

Net Grocer, www.netgrocer.com, online grocery store.

Netcheck Commerce Bureau, www.netcheck.com, an alternative to the Better Business Bureau offering online merchant services and facilitating the resolution of complaints on any web site concerning fraud, refunds, copyright infringement, false advertising, and spam; includes a global consumer complaint search engine.

NetworkSolutions, www.networksolutions.com, web hosting, domain name registration.

No More Cookies, www.nomorecookies.com, software that tracks and controls cookies on your computer.

Office Depot, www.officedepot.com, office equipment, furniture, supplies.

OfficeMax, www.officemax.com, office equipment, furniture, supplies.

OnGuard Online, www.onguardonline.gov, tips from the federal government and technology industry to guard against internet fraud, secure your computer, and protect your personal information.

Orbitz, www.orbitz.com, online travel site.

Orlando Real Estate, www.orlandorealestate.com, site of RE/MAX real estate brokers Jerry and Irene Stoffer.

Overstock Auctions, http://auctions.overstock.com, Overstock.com's auction site which can also be access from the home page of www.overstock.com.

PayPal, www.paypal.com, online payment service.

Petsmart, www.petsmart.com, pet toys and supplies.

PlanetFeedback, www.planetfeedback.com, a consumer feedback site.

PowerSnipe, www.powersnipe.com, auction sniping software.

PriceGrabber.com, www.pricegrabber.com, online comparison shopping site.

Purchasing, www.purchasing.com, the site of *Purchasing Magazine.*

Quicken Loans, www.quickenloans.com, home loans.

QuikDrop, www.quikdrop.com, a franchised eBay trading assistant/ trading post that operates in storefronts across the United States and sells items on eBay for individuals who don't want to do it themselves.

QVC, www.qvc.com, electronic retailer.

RebatesHQ, www.rebateshq.com, find and track rebates.

Red Envelope, www.redenvelope.com, gifts.

Reed Link, www.reedlink.com, the manufacturing product search engine of Reed Business Information.

Rent.com, www.rent.com, apartment and home rentals, roommate matching services.

RentNet, www.rentnet.com, online apartment rental guide.

Rip-off Report.com, www.ripoffreport.com, a site where consumers can post details of problems with companies.

Roommates.com, www.roommates.com, roommate matching service.

Scambusters, www.scambusters.com, resource for information about online scams.

School Report, www.theschoolreport.com, information on school districts.

ShopLocal, www.shoplocal.com, site that lets you find local merchants.

Shoppers Resource, www.shoppersresource.com, coupons, rebates, promotional codes.

Shopping.com, www.shopping.com, online comparison shopping site owned by eBay.

Shopzilla, www.shopzilla.com, shopping search engine.

SmarterTravel, www.smartertravel.com, online travel site.

Snopes, www.snopes.com, a site that researches and provides details on urban legends and internet hoaxes.

Spam Stock Tracker, www.spamstocktracker.com, site that demonstrates how much money can be lost by buying stocks promoted by spam e-mails.

SpywareRemoversReview, www.spywareremoversreview.com, reviews and compares spyware removal software.

Square Trade, www.squaretrade.com, merchant verification, post-purchase protection, online dispute resolution.

Staples, www.staples.com, office equipment, furniture, supplies.

Susan G. Komen Breast Cancer Foundation, www.komen.org, a nonprofit foundation with a mission to fight breast cancer through its support of research and community-based outreach programs; the site includes information, opportunities to donate, and a gift shop with a variety of pink ribbon products.

Symantec's Hoax Page, www.symantec.com/avcenter/hoax.html, identifies e-mail hoaxes.

Thomas Net, www.thomasnet.com, an industrial search engine and provider of internet marketing solutions.

TicketLiquidator, www.ticketliquidator.com, event tickets.

TicketMaster, www.ticketmaster.com, event tickets.

TicketsNow, www.ticketsnow.com, event tickets.

Travel Guard International, www.travelguard.com, travel insurance that covers vacation and trip cancellation, travel interruptions and delays, emergency medical and health expenses, lost baggage, and more.

Travelocity, www.travelocity.com, online travel site.

Tripod, www.tripod.com, free and fee-based web hosting, blogging (part of the Lycos network).

TruthOrFiction, www.truthorfiction.com, a site that checks out internet rumors, inspirational stores, virus warnings, pleas for help, and calls to action to determine if they are truth or fiction.

U.S. Customs and Border Protection, www.cbp.gov, U.S. import information.

U.S. Department of State, www.state.gov, includes information about passports and visas, travel warnings, consular information sheets, and public announcements.

U.S. Department of Transportation, www.dot.gov, includes information about travel and transportation services in the United States.

WebAssured, www.webassured.com, offers independent web site certification and free online dispute resolution service.

Westlaw, www.westlaw.com, subscription-based online legal research service.

Yahoo!, www.yahoo.com, search engine, shopping, auctions, discussion groups, and more.

Yahoo! Auctions, http://auctions.shopping.yahoo.com, Yahoo!'s auction site which can also be accessed from the home page of www.yahoo.com.

List of Web Sites by Categories

(some sites may appear in more than one category)

Auction Sniping

AuctionBlitz, www.auctionblitz.com, auction sniping software.

AuctionSniper, www.auctionsniper.com, auction sniping software.

eSnipe, www.esnipe.com, auction sniping software.

PowerSnipe, www.powersnipe.com, auction sniping software.

Automotive

Autobytel Inc., www.autobytel.com, an internet automotive marketing services company offering new and used car pricing and information.

AutoCheck, www.autocheck.com, vehicle history reports for used cars.

AutoWeb, www.autoweb.com, a third-party automotive e-commerce site offering pricing and other information.

Capital One Auto Finance, www.capitaloneautofinance.com, automobile loans.

Car and Driver, www.caranddriver.com, the web site of *Car and Driver* magazine.

CarBuyingTips, www.carbuyingtips.com, advice on car buying, leasing, and avoiding dealer scams.

Carfax, www.carfax.com, vehicle history reports for used cars.

Edmunds.com Inc., www.edmunds.com, new and used automotive pricing, vehicle reviews, and other information about the automobile purchase process.

Lending Tree, www.lendingtree.com, mortgage, auto, and other loans.

Business: Sites of Interest to Business Owners

Kelly Search, www.kellysearch.com, an industrial product and service search engine featuring a global database of companies.

Office Depot, www.officedepot.com, office equipment, furniture, supplies.

OfficeMax, www.officemax.com, office equipment, furniture, supplies.

Purchasing, www.purchasing.com, the site of *Purchasing* magazine.

Reed Link, www.reedlink.com, the manufacturing product search engine of Reed Business Information.

Staples, www.staples.com, office equipment, furniture, supplies.

Thomas Net, www.thomasnet.com, an industrial search engine and provider of internet marketing solutions.

Consumer Information and Services

Amazon.com, www.amazon.com, a retail site selling books, music, and a wide range of other consumer products that allows consumers to review and rank the items it sells.

Better Business Bureau, www.bbb.org, a network of agencies that collects and provides information about companies.

Better Business Bureau Online, www.bbbonline.org, a site of the Better Business Bureau focused on promoting trust and confidence on the internet.

BizRate, www.bizrate.com, consumer feedback site operated by Shopzilla.

CNET, www.cnet.com, professional and consumer product reviews and price comparisons for technology-related products.

Complaints.com, www.complaints.com, a database of personal, first-hand, consumer experiences with products and services.

Consumer Action Website, www.consumeraction.gov, consumer information.

Consumer Reports, www.consumerreports.org, the web site for the popular consumer magazine.

Consumerreview.com, www.consumerreview.com, provides reviews, advice, and shopping opportunities for outdoor sporting goods and consumer electronics.

ConsumerSearch, www.consumersearch.com, gathers and analyzes product reviews and offers a list of top-rated products.

ConsumerWorld.org, www.consumerworld.org, a guide of consumer resources.

Epinions, www.epinions.com, offers product reviews and recommendations, plus links to merchants.

ePublicEye.com, www.epubliceye.com, a site that allows consumers to rate e-businesses for reliability, privacy, and customer satisfaction.

FBI's Internet Fraud Complaint Center, www.ifccfbi.gov, a resource for information about internet crimes and a place to file a complaint if you have been a victim.

Federal Trade Commission, www.ftc.gov, the United States consumer protection agency.

GetNetWise, www.getnetwise.org, a collaborative effort of a broad-based coalition of companies, public interest organizations, non-profits, and trade associations with information to show internet users how to stay safe and secure online.

National Association of Boards of Pharmacy (NABP), www.nabp.net, a professional association representing state boards of pharmacy in the United States and certain other countries.

National Fraud Information Center, www.fraud.org, information on internet and telemarketing fraud.

Netcheck Commerce Bureau, www.netcheck.com, an alternative to the Better Business Bureau offering online merchant services and facilitating the resolution of complaints on any web site concerning fraud, refunds, copyright infringement, false advertising, and spam; includes a global consumer complaint search engine.

OnGuard Online, www.onguardonline.gov, tips from the federal government and technology industry to guard against internet fraud, secure your computer, and protect your personal information.

PlanetFeedback, www.planetfeedback.com, a consumer feedback site.

Rip-off Report.com, www.ripoffreport.com, a site where consumers can post details of problems with companies.

Scambusters, www.scambusters.com, resource for information about online scams.

Square Trade, www.squaretrade.com, merchant verification, post-purchase protection, online dispute resolution.

WebAssured, www.webassured.com, offers independent web site certification and free online dispute resolution service.

Coupons and Rebates

Able Shoppers, www.ableshoppers.com, specials and coupons.

CoolSavings, www.coolsavings.com, online and printable coupons.

Coupon Cabin, www.couponcabin.com, online coupons and promotional codes.

CouponMountain, www.couponmountain.com, free coupons.

Current Codes, www.currentcodes.com, discount and coupon codes.

Deal Catcher, www.dealcatcher.com, store ads, coupons, specials.

Deal Hunting, www.dealhunting.com, coupons and great deals.

Deal Taker, www.dealtaker.com, coupons and special deals.

FatWallet, www.fatwallet.com, source for online coupons, bargain shopping, and price comparisons.

Hot Deals Club, www.hotdealsclub.com, online deals, coupons, promotions.

My Rebates, www.myrebates.com, find and buy products with rebates, track rebates.

RebatesHQ, www.rebateshq.com, find and track rebates.

Shoppers Resource, www.shoppersresource.com, coupons, rebates, promotional codes.

Data Protection and Computer Security

Cookie Central, www.cookiecentral.com, information and news about cookies.

Download.com, www.download.com, offers a wide variety of downloadable software, including free and for-pay spyware removal programs, plus free and trial offers from various software companies.

GeoTrust, www.geotrust.com, digital certificate provider offering online transaction security, identity verification, and trust services.

No More Cookies, www.nomorecookies.com, software that tracks and controls cookies on your computer.

SpywareRemoversReview, www.spywareremoversreview.com, reviews and compares spyware removal software.

Symantec's Hoax Page, www.symantec.com/avcenter/hoax.html, identifies e-mail hoaxes.

Dating and Introduction Services

eHarmony, www.eharmony.com, online introduction and dating service.

Great Expectations, www.great-expectations.com, online introduction and dating service.

Match.com, www.match.com, online introduction and dating service.

Domain Name Registrars and Web Hosting

GeoCities, www.geocities.com, free and fee-based web hosting (a Yahoo! service).

GoDaddy, www.godaddy.com, domain name registration, transfer, hosting.

NetworkSolutions, www.networksolutions.com, web hosting, domain name registration.

Tripod, www.tripod.com, free and fee-based web hosting, blogging (part of the Lycos network).

Financial Information and Services

AnnualCreditReport, www.annualcreditreport.com, a centralized service for consumers to request free annual credit reports.

Bankrate, www.bankrate.com, online financial rate information.

Bidpay, www.bidpay.com, online auction payment service.

Capital One Auto Finance, www.capitaloneautofinance.com, automobile loans.

E-Loan, www.eloan.com, mortgage, auto, and personal loans.

Federal Deposit Insurance Corporation (FDIC), www.fdic.gov, supervises banks and insures deposits.

Freecreditreport, www.freecreditreport.com, a commercial site of Experian, a credit reporting agency that offers a free copy of your credit report when you sign up for a trial membership in its monthly credit monitoring service; do not confuse this site with www.annualcreditreport.com, where you can get a no-strings-attached free copy of your credit report.

InsWeb, www.insweb.com, online insurance marketplace for automobile, term life, homeowners, renters, and individual health insurance products.

InvestorGuide.com, www.investorguide.com, information about investing and finance.

Lending Tree, www.lendingtree.com, mortgage, auto, and other loans.

PayPal, www.paypal.com, online payment service.

Quicken Loans, www.quickenloans.com, home loans.

Spam Stock Tracker, www.spamstocktracker.com, site that demonstrates how much money can be lost by buying stocks promoted by spam e-mails.

Food and Recipes

Allrecipes.com, www.allrecipes.com, features recipes and allows users to rank and comment on recipes.

Busy Moms Recipes, www.busymomsrecipes.com, easy-to-prepare recipes and monthly newsletter.

Epicurious, www.epicurious.com, features recipes, links to sites selling fine foods and specialty items, gourmet travel packages.

Gift Cards

CardAvenue.com, www.cardavenue.com, buy, sell, and trade gift cards.

CertificateSwap.com, www.certificateswap.com, a gift certificate marketplace that allows consumers to purchase or sell gift certificates.

Gift Card Guide, www.gift-card-guide.com, information and news about gift cards.

GiftCardBuyBack.com, www.giftcardbuyback.com, buy, sell, and trade gift cards.

GiftCardsAgain.com, www.giftcardsagain.com, buy, sell, and trade gift cards.

Government Agencies and Web Sites

Centers for Disease Control Travelers' Health page, www.cdc.gov/travel, information for specific destinations, vaccination information, advice for dealing with injury or illness abroad, and travel health warnings and notices.

FBI's Internet Fraud Complaint Center, www.ifccfbi.gov, a resource for information about internet crimes and a place to file a complaint if you have been a victim.

Federal Deposit Insurance Corporation (FDIC), www.fdic.gov, supervises banks and insures deposits.

Federal Trade Commission, www.ftc.gov, the United States consumer protection agency.

Hoaxbusters, http://hoaxbusters.ciac.org/, the U.S. Department of Energy's site on internet hoaxes.

OnGuard Online, www.onguardonline.gov, tips from the federal government and technology industry to guard against internet fraud, secure your computer, and protect your personal information.

U.S. Customs and Border Protection, www.cbp.gov, U.S. import information.

U.S. Department of State, www.state.gov, includes information about passports and visas, travel warnings, consular information sheets, and public announcements.

U.S. Department of Transportation, www.dot.gov, includes information about travel and transportation services in the United States.

Internet Hoaxes and Urban Legends

About Urban Legends and Folklore, http://urbanlegends.about.com, a site that researches and provides details on urban legends, internet hoaxes, and netlore.

Hoaxbusters, http://hoaxbusters.ciac.org/, the U.S. Department of Energy's site on internet hoaxes.

Scambusters, www.scambusters.com, resource for information about online scams.

Snopes, www.snopes.com, a site that researches and provides details on urban legends and internet hoaxes.

TruthOrFiction, www.truthorfiction.com, a site that checks out internet rumors, inspirational stores, virus warnings, pleas for help, and calls to action to determine if they are truth or fiction.

Job Search Sites

Career Journal, www.careerjournal.com, the *Wall Street Journal*'s executive career site.

CareerBuilder, www.careerbuilder.com, job search and employment site.

Hotjobs, www.hotjobs.com, Yahoo!'s job search site.

Job-Hunt.org, www.job-hunt.org, online job search guide and resource directory.

Monster, www.monster.com, job search and employment site.

Online Auction and Related Sites

AuctionBlitz, www.auctionblitz.com, auction sniping software.

AuctionSniper, www.auctionsniper.com, auction sniping software.

Bidpay, www.bidpay.com, online auction payment service.

Online Shopper's

Bidville, www.bidville.com, online auction site.

Bidz.com, www.bidz.com, online auction site.

eBay Inc., www.ebay.com, worldwide online marketplace where users buy and sell in auction and fixed price formats.

eSnipe, www.esnipe.com, www.powersnipe.com.

Overstock Auctions, http://auctions.overstock.com, Overstock.com's auction site that can also be accessed from the home page of www.overstock.com.

PayPal, www.paypal.com, online payment service.

QuikDrop, www.quikdrop.com, an eBay trading assistant/trading post that operates in storefronts across the United States and sells items on eBay for individuals who don't want to do it themselves.

Yahoo! Auctions, http://auctions.shopping.yahoo.com, Yahoo!'s auction site which can also be accessed from the home page of www.yahoo.com.

Publications

Consumer Reports, www.consumerreports.org, the web site for the popular consumer magazine.

Purchasing, www.purchasing.com, the site of *Purchasing* magazine.

Real Estate Sales and Rentals

Apartments.com, www.apartments.com, nationwide apartment search site.

National Association of Realtors®, www.realtor.com, information on finding and buying a home, rentals, financing, moving, and more.

Orlando Real Estate, www.orlandorealestate.com, site of RE/MAX real estate brokers Jerry and Irene Stoffer.

Rent.com, www.rent.com, apartment and home rentals, roommate matching services.

RentNet, www.rentnet.com, online apartment rental guide.

Roommates.com, www.roommates.com, roommate matching service.

School Report, www.theschoolreport.com, information on school districts.

Retail

Amazon.com, www.amazon.com, a retail site selling books, music, and
a wide range of other consumer products that allows consumers to
review and rank the items it sells.

Costco, www.costco.com, Costco Wholesale's online store.

DogToys.com, www.dogtoys.com, pet toys and supplies.

Gifts.com, www.gifts.com, gifts.

Net Grocer, www.netgrocer.com, online grocery store.

Petsmart, www.petsmart.com, pet toys and supplies.

QuikDrop, www.quikdrop.com, an eBay trading assistant/trading post
that operates in storefronts across the United States and sells items
on eBay for individuals who don't want to do it themselves.

QVC, www.qvc.com, electronic retailer.

Red Envelope, www.redenvelope.com, gifts.

Susan G. Komen Breast Cancer Foundation, www.komen.org, a nonprofit
foundation with a mission to fight breast cancer through its support
of research and community-based outreach programs; the site
includes information, opportunities to donate, and a gift shop with
a variety of pink ribbon products.

Search Engines

AltaVista, www.altavista.com, search engine, shopping, travel, and more.

Ask Jeeves, www.askjeeves.com, search engine, shopping, and more.

Dogpile, www.dogpile.com, general search engine that searches other
major search engine sites.

Google, www.google.com, search engine, shopping.

iVillage, www.ivillage.com, describes itself as "the internet for
women," includes a search engine, discussion boards, and more.

LexisNexis, www.lexisnexis.com, subscription-based search engine for
legal, news, and business information.

Lycos, www.lycos.com, general search engine, web hosting, blogging, discussion groups, and more.

Westlaw, www.westlaw.com, subscription-based online legal research service.

Yahoo!, www.yahoo.com, search engine, shopping, auctions, discussion groups, and more.

Shopping and Price Comparison

AltaVista, www.altavista.com, search engine, shopping, travel, and more.

Amazon.com, www.amazon.com, a retail site selling books, music, and a wide range of other consumer products that allows consumers to review and rank the items it sells.

Ask Jeeves, www.askjeeves.com, search engine, shopping, and more.

CNET, www.cnet.com, professional and consumer product reviews and price comparisons for technology-related products.

Froogle, www.froogle,com, Google's shopping site.

Google, www.google.com, search engine, shopping.

Internet Shopper, www.internetshopper.com, comparison site for products, prices, and merchants.

My Personal Shopper, www.mypersonalshopper.com, personal shopping service.

PriceGrabber.com, www.pricegrabber.com, online comparison shopping site.

ShopLocal, www.shoplocal.com, site that lets you find local merchants.

Shopping.com, www.shopping.com, online comparison shopping site owned by eBay.

Shopzilla, www.shopzilla.com, shopping search engine.

Yahoo!, www.yahoo.com, search engine, shopping, auctions, discussion groups, and more.

Tickets

TicketLiquidator, www.ticketliquidator.com, event tickets.

TicketMaster, www.ticketmaster.com, event tickets.

TicketsNow, www.ticketsnow.com, event tickets.

Travel

AltaVista, www.altavista.com, search engine, shopping, travel, and more.

Centers for Disease Control Travelers' Health page, www.cdc.gov/travel, information for specific destinations, vaccination information, advice for dealing with injury or illness abroad, and travel health warnings and notices.

Expedia.com, www.expedia.com, online travel site.

Hotel Discounts, www.hoteldiscounts.com, discounted hotel accommodations.

Orbitz, www.orbitz.com, online travel site.

SmarterTravel, www.smartertravel.com, online travel site.

Travel Guard International, www.travelguard.com, travel insurance that covers vacation and trip cancellation, travel interruptions and delays, emergency medical and health expenses, lost baggage, and more.

Travelocity, www.travelocity.com, online travel site.

U.S. Customs and Border Protection, www.cbp.gov, U.S. import information.

U.S. Department of State, www.state.gov, includes information about passports and visas, travel warnings, consular information sheets, and public announcements.

U.S. Department of Transportation, www.dot.gov, includes information about travel and transportation services in the United States.

Glossary

Adware. Software that automatically plays, displays, or downloads advertising material to a computer.

Affiliate. A web site, company, or marketing program that attempts to drive traffic to a particular web site via a link on another site.

Auction. A public sale of property or merchandise to the highest bidder.

Bit. The smallest element of computerized data.

Bookmark. A file within a browser that allows a user to save the addresses of interesting or frequently used web sites.

Brick-and-mortar. Located in or serving customers from a physical facility, as opposed to an online operation.

Browser. A software application used to locate and display web pages; also called web browser.

Browser hijacker. A common spyware program that changes the home page of a web browser, even though the user changes it back.

Bulletin board. An area of a web site where users post messages for other users.

Cache. A file on a computer's hard drive in which a web browser stores information such as addresses, text, and graphics from recently-visited web sites.

Chat. A feature offered by many online services or web sites that allows users to communicate by typing messages that are displayed almost instantly on the screens of other participants in the chat room.

Chat room. The name of a place or page in a web site or online service where people can chat using instant messages.

Click-and-mortar. Refers to a store that exists online and in the physical world.

Cookie. A small data file created by a web server that is stored on your hard drive either temporarily or permanently and provides a way for web sites to identify users and track their preferences.

Cyberspace. Refers to the resources available and the culture that is developing in electronically connected communities; the term is also used to distinguish the physical world from the digital or computer-based world.

Data mining. The practice of compiling information about internet users by tracking and recording their activities on web sites.

Digital wallet. Encryption software that works much like a physical wallet during e-commerce transactions, securely storing a user's payment information.

Discussion group. An online area, such as an electronic bulletin board, where users can read and post comments about specific topics.

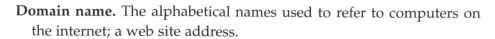
Domain name. The alphabetical names used to refer to computers on the internet; a web site address.

E-mail spoofing. Forging the sender's address on an e-mail to make it appear as if it came from someone other than the actual source.

Encryption. The process of obscuring information to make it unreadable without special knowledge; in contemporary usage, refers to the reversible transformation of data from its original form to a difficult-to-interpret format as a mechanism for protecting its confidentiality, integrity, and sometimes its authenticity.

Escrow service. A licensed and regulated company that collects, holds, and sends a buyer's money to a seller according to instructions agreed on by both the buyer and seller.

FAQ (frequently asked questions). Pages which list and answer the questions most often asked about a web site, company, product, etc.

Financial information. Information about an individual's finances, including account status, balance, payment history, and information about an individual's purchase history and use of financial instruments including credit and debit card information.

Firewall. A barrier that protects a computer or network from anyone who tries to access it from outside without authorization.

Gift card. A pre-paid card offered by a retailer or financial institution in lieu of a traditional gift certificate.

Hacker. Someone who breaks into your computer or into a network of computers over the internet without permission; a hacker's purpose may or may not be malicious.

Hidden dialers. Programs that are often downloaded without the user's knowledge that use a computer to silently dial expensive phone calls that later show up on your telephone bill.

Home page. The first page of a web site that introduces the site and provides the means of navigation.

HTTP (hypertext transfer protocol). The standard language that computers connected to the World Wide Web use to communicate with each other.

Hyperlink. An image or portion of text on a web page that is linked to another web page, either on the same site or on another web site; clicking on a hyperlink will take the user to another web page or another place on the same page.

Identity theft. When someone uses the personal information of another without permission to commit fraud or other crimes; identity theft is the fastest-growing internet crime.

Individual profiling. Refers to a site's or service provider's use of personal data to create or build a record on a particular user, typically for marketing purposes.

Insurance. A device for indemnifying or guaranteeing an individual against loss; in the context of online shopping, insurance protects buyers and sellers against items that may be lost or damaged in shipping.

Internet. An interconnected system of networks that connects millions of computers around the world via the TCP/IP protocol.

Internet service provider (ISP). A company that provides access to the internet; also called internet access providers (IAP).

Keystroke logger. Hardware or software that records each keystroke made on a particular computer; can be used as a tool for parents to monitor children's computer activities but may also be used for malicious purposes.

Keyword. A word that is entered into the search form or search window of a search engine to search the World Wide Web for pages or sites about or including the keyword and information related to it.

Mailing list. An e-mail-based discussion forum dedicated to a particular topic of interest.

Malware. *Mal*icious soft*ware*, typically designed to damage or disrupt a system, to track the user's activities, or to take control of the computer.

Navigation. A system of hypertext paths set up on a web page that enables visitors to find their way around the site.

Netiquette. The informal rules of internet courtesy.

Netizens. Citizens of cyberspace.

Newsgroups. Discussion groups on the internet classified by subject matter.

Online payment service. A company that facilitates the transfer of funds from a customer to an online seller; the money may come from the buyer's bank account, credit card, or another funding source.

Opt-in. A policy for giving permission under which the user explicitly permits the web site operator to collect information, use it in a specified manner, and/or share it with others when such use or disclosure to third parties is unrelated to the purpose for which the information was collected; you allow the web site operator to use your information by opting-in.

Opt-out. A policy under which the user's permission for data collection and/or sharing is implied unless the user explicitly requests that the information not be collected, used, and/or shared when such use or disclosure to third parties is unrelated to the purpose for which the information was collected; unless you deny permission by opting-out, the web site operator can use your information.

Phishing. Pronounced "fishing;" sending an e-mail that falsely claims to represent an established enterprise in an effort to scam the recipient into providing private information that can be used for identity theft purposes.

Pop-up ads (or "pop-ups"). A term used for unsolicited advertising that appears as its own browser window.

Privacy policy. The policy under which the company or organization operating a web site handles the personal information collected about visitors to the site.

Real estate. Land and any buildings or structures permanently affixed to it.

Scumware. Malicious code that changes how you view the web sites you visit by replacing the actual content of sites with ads from scumware advertisers.

Search engine. A tool used to located information on the World Wide Web.

Secondary use. Refers to using personal information collected for one purpose for a second, unrelated purpose.

Server. A special computer connected to a network that provides (serves up) data; a server may also be called a host or node.

Shipping and handling. A phrase that usually refers to the amount a merchant charges to package and ship a product.

Shopping cart. Software that handles an online store's ordering process, allowing customers to select merchandise, review their orders, make modifications or additions, and complete their purchases.

Spam. Unsolicited commercial e-mail.

Spamming. Sending off-topic, unsolicited, and inappropriate messages in bulk quantities.

Spider. A software program that "crawls" the web, searching and indexing web pages to create a database that can be easily searched by a search engine.

Spyware. Software that covertly gathers information and activity on a computer without the user's knowledge.

Surfing. The activity of casually and randomly looking at something that offers numerous options, such as the internet or television (web surfing, channel surfing).

Trojan horse. A malicious program that is disguised as something benign.

URL (uniform resource locator). The World Wide Web address of a site on the internet.

Virus. A malicious computer program designed to replicate itself by copying itself into the other programs stored in a computer.

Web site. An organization's or individual's presence on the internet; a collection of web pages linked to each other and including a home page hosted on a server by its owner or at an ISP.

Webmaster. The person responsible for administering a web site.

Window. An enclosed rectangular space on a computer screen.

World Wide Web. A system of internet servers that support specially formatted documents; not all internet servers are part of the World Wide Web.

Worm. A self-replicating malicious computer program, similar to a computer virus, which is self-contained and does not need to be part of another program to propagate itself.

Index

A

Abbreviations, common online, 162

ABCs of evaluating sites, 12–13

Account information, protecting your, 90–91

Advertising, legitimate site, 16

Affiliate programs, 16

After-sale service and support, 14

Alcoholic beverages, online buying of, 73–74

Appendix, online shopping resources, 173–193

Auctions, online. *See* Online auctions

B

Better Business Bureau reports, 16–18

Brick-and-mortar stores, occasions for choosing, 31

Business supplies, online buying of, 153–154

Buyer protection programs, online, 88

Buying venues and methods, overview of online, 8–9

C

Cars, online buying of, 125–130 shopping tips, 127

Chain e-mails, 106–109

sample of, 108
College savings plan, 151
Consumer protection
    issues, 35, 79–96
    services, online, 15
Consumer review sites, 19
Contact information, offline, 13
Cookies, 94–95
Coupons, online, 29
Credit card
    billing errors, 87–88
    payment as safest method for
        online shopping, 81–82
Customer endorsements, 16

D

Damages, claiming, 27–28
Dating, online, 159–163
    safety precautions for, 161, 163
Defective merchandise, 86
Domain suffixes, understanding, 20

E

E-commerce, evolution of, 6
E-mail address, online shopping,
    80–81
eBay. *See* Online auctions
Electronic devices, securing all of
    your, 95–96
Entertainment, online buying of,
    143–144
Error messages, web site, 22
Escrow accounts
    and online fraud, 121–123
    when to use, 120–121

F

Fake money order scam, 104–106
Financial services, online, 151–153
Finding what you want online, 63–69
Foreign countries, buying from, 75–77

customs, duty and taxes, 77
payment and foreign currency, 76
shipping, 76–77
Forums, message boards, discussion
    boards and lists for sharing com-
    mon interests, 156–159
Frauds and scams, 35, 97–115
    identity theft, 98–100
    online auction, 40–41
    steps for testing the transaction,
        110
    tips for avoiding, 111–113
    what to do if you have been a vic-
        tim of, 113–115
Future of online shopping, 171–172

G

Generational issues, 33–35
Gift cards/certificates, 149–151
Gift registries, pros and cons of, 148
Gift giving, online, 147–148
Glossary, 195–201
Gourmet food, online buying of,
    146–147
Groceries, online buying of, 146–147

H

Hidden price inflators, 14–15
High-priced merchandise, buying,
    123
History of mail order shopping, 4–6
Hoaxes, 106–109
    sample of, 108

I

Identity theft, 98–100
Identity thieves, safeguarding
    against, 91–96. *See also* Frauds and
    scams, Identity theft
Illegal items, online offerings of, 72
Insuring your shipment, 27–28

J

Jewelry, online buying of high-priced, 120–121

Job seeking, online, 164–165

K

Keylogger programs, thwarting, 92

L

Let's go shopping, 39–56

Link alteration, 104

Local shopping, 69

Lost shipments, 85–86

M

Malicious software and code, various forms of, 09, 93–96

Manufacturer rebates, 29

Money-saving tips, online shopping, 28–31

N

Non-drivers, online shopping for, 7

O

Online auctions

and prohibited items, 72

avoiding bidding wars, 60

before placing a bid, 51–52

bidding process, 52–54

favorites, bookmarking, 47–48

feedback ratings, 55, 58–59

good, bad and bargains of, 57–62

how they work, 39–42

imitating techniques of other bidders, 46–47

"last second" bidding, 54–55

misspellings in titles, using to your advantage in, 46

mistakes, yours, not the sellers, 61

overview of, 39–42

photographs of items, 50–51

problem resolution, 61

seller status, 48–50, 58–59

shadowing bidders during, 46–47

user IDs, 60

when things go wrong, 56

Orders not shipped on time or at all, 85. *See also* Shipping

P

Payment options for online purchases, 23–25, 81–83

Payment transfer scams, 163–164, 165–167. *See also* Frauds and scams

Personal information, guarding your, 89–90, 91. *See also* Frauds and scams, Identity theft

Pet medications and supplies, online buying of, 145–146

Phishing scams, 91, 101–104

Pieces and parts, online availability of product, 147

Pop-up screens, 91

Prescription medication, 144–145

Price inflators, hidden, 14–15

Print catalog, coordinating with company web site, 68

Privacy policy, 15

Problems

common, 85–87

rectifying, 83–85

Product

descriptions, 14

reviews, 18–19

Purchasing process, 20–23

Q

QVC Queen, 28

R

Real estate, shopping online for, 131–135

a home to buy, 133
buying through auctions, 134
rentals, 132–133
timeshare and vacation rentals,
134–135
Recipes and cooking tips, 147
Recordkeeping, 89
Red flags, 18
Refund and return policies, 14
Regulations, federal, state and local,
83
Reviews, site, 18–19

S
Sales tax, 25–26
Sales, specials, rebates, discounts,
online shopping, 28–31
Scams. *See* Frauds and scams
Scumware, 92
Search engines
definition of, 65
how they work, 64–66
how to use online, 66–67
keywords, modifiers, and quotes,
67–68
shopping the shopping, 68
Sears Catalog, 5
Secure payments, 81–83
Security, importance of computer,
91–96
Sellers, evaluating online, 12, 18
Seniors and online shopping, 35
Shipping
agent scam, 104–106
overview of online, 7–8
policy, 26–27
problems, 85–86
reduced, 30
Shopping basics, online, 11–31
Site connections, difficulty with, 22

Spam
never buy anything from unso-
licited e-mail, 73, 101 (*See also*
Frauds and scams)
Spoofing, 101–104
Spyware, 92–96
Staying safe online, information for,
80

T
Tobacco products, online buying of,
73
Travel services, online, 137–141
drawbacks of, 141
valuable information for, 140

U
Unresponsive retailers, 86–87
Unwanted merchandise, 86
Upselling, resisting unnecessary, 90
User-friendly sites, 12–16

W
Warranty information, 89
Weapons, online buying of, 73
Web sites
alphabetical list of, 173–182
categorical list of, 182–93
evaluating, 12–16

Y
Young people and online shopping,
33–34